Table of Contents

Disclaimer

The information provided in this book is designed to provide helpful information on the subjects discussed. This book is not meant to be used, nor should it be used, to diagnose or treat any medical condition. For diagnosis or treatment of any medical problem, consult your own physician. The publisher and author are not responsible for any specific health or allergy needs that may require medical supervision and are not liable for any damages or negative consequences from any treatment, action, application or preparation, to any person reading or following the information in this book. References are provided for informational purposes only and do not constitute endorsement of any websites or other sources. Readers should be aware that the websites listed in this book may change.

I recommend consulting a doctor to assess and/or identify any health related issues prior to making any dramatic changes to your diet.

About the Author

Scott James has been addicted to all things fitness, health and nutrition for nearly a decade.

With a large amount of hype surrounding the fitness industry, as well as the dieting and supplementation niches Scott thought it was the right time to come forward and debunk the myths and scams within the industry.

All information conveyed in Scott's books is tried and tested - no false hope or bad information is shared.

Scott believes that when an individual is equipped with the correct knowledge and a plan of action that he will provide in his books they are unstoppable.

Scott is not here to make money, he's here to make a different and guide you on your journey to unlocking the new, better you.

Bonus Content

As a token of my appreciation, I'd like to give you access to my exclusive bonus content.

Here's what you're about to receive...

•   The Bodyweight Barrage eBook - the ultimate guide to building muscle and shredding fat without a gym, including exercise descriptions, photos and more!

•   Immediate email access to me, SJ. Ask me anything, and I'll give you an answer

•   My honest product reviews and recommendations

In order to claim your bonus content, simply navigate to:

http://ignorelimits.com/

Enter your email in the box so you can receive this exclusive content instantly!

As this is a limited time offer I recommend claiming your Bodyweight Barrage ebook before proceeding to read the book.

Introduction

Cooking - it's either something you love or something you hate, and funnily enough this perception is more often than not based on your cooking abilities! As a health and fitness advocate I have spent endless hours in the kitchen trying to follow complex recipes with obscure ingredients and utensils I didn't have to create bland meals I didn't enjoy.

If you are on a 'diet' or trying to gain lean muscle you will more than likely have gone through a phase of desensitizing yourself to foods, don't worry I went through that stage too! Cooking is meant to be fun, after several years of trial and error in the kitchen I have compiled 160 of my favorite muscle building and fat burning recipes that are easy to make and don't require any complex ingredients or utensils.

The recipes within this book include breakfasts, main meals, snacks and desserts, protein smoothies and sides. All of these meals are loaded with flavour, and even better they are loaded with protein and nutrients. Every recipe has the total number of calories along with a macronutrient breakdown stating the amount of protein, carbohydrates and fats per serve (measured in grams).

If you're anything like me you'll have a sweet tooth for berry pancakes, Boston cream donuts and a variety of other mouth-watering sweet foods. In this book I will show you how to EASILY make these and be able to incorporate them into your diet DAILY if you wish while still achieving your fat loss/muscle gain goals.

It's time to debunk the 'clean eating' myth!

The IIFYM Flexible Dieting Cookbook Explained

First of all, let's clarify flexible dieting. Flexible dieting is more of a lifestyle then an actual diet. Flexible dieting eliminates 'clean' and 'dirty' foods and instead focuses on the bigger picture – your daily caloric needs. Flexible dieting thrives off the principle that a calorie is a calorie and which source it comes from will have no effect on body composition. You can gain fat eating 'clean' foods if you exceed the daily amount of calories your body requires just like you can lose fat eating 'dirty' foods as long as the total calories consumed are below that of your maintenance level.

IIFYM, short for 'If it Fits Your Macros' refers to choosing foods that fit your daily macronutrient goal.

This cookbook contains a plethora of delicious recipes, all with macronutrient breakdowns; therefore you know exactly how many grams of protein, carbohydrates and fat are within each recipe along with the total caloric number that you can then use to reach your caloric goal for the day.

Calories & Macronutrients Explained

So what is a calorie?

A calorie is an energy source, humans require calories in order to maintain life. We are constantly trying to increase and decrease our caloric intake based on our goals such as: whether we want to slim down, gain lean muscle mass or perform a certain way for sports. If a calorie that is consumed is not utilised it will be converted by the body and stored as fat – this calorie could be from a stick of celery or a scoop of ice cream, it is irrelevant.

Calories can come from several different macronutrient sources, these include:

Protein – 4 calories per gram– protein is the building block for lean muscle mass.

Carbohydrates – 4 calories per gram – carbohydrates are used by our bodies as the primary energy source. Carbohydrates are broken down into 2 sub categories (both contain 4 cal/gram).

Simple carbohydrates – these are the sugary processed carbohydrates that are found in foods such as lollies, chocolate and fruit. Simple carbohydrates are absorbed quickly and cause a large insulin spike.

Complex carbohydrates – These carbohydrates are the 'clean' slow digesting carbohydrates that are known for sustained energy. Complex carbs are found in brown rice, sweet potato and oats.

Fat – 9 calories per gram – Healthy fats are vital for bodily functions such as hormone levels. Fats are also broken down into several categories:

Saturated fat – found in dairy and meat, can raise cholesterol.

Unsatured fat – found in vegetable oils, used to lower cholesterol.

Alcohol – 7 calories per gram – empty calories (alcohol does not contain any macronutrients).

Calculating your Macronutrient Requirement

In order to begin your flexible diet you need to know your daily caloric goal! In order to calculate this goal the following formula is used, please note the slight variation in formula for men and women:

Based on the extremely accurate Mifflin - St Jeor equation

MEN: BMR = [9.99 x weight (kg)] + [6.25 x height (cm)] - [4.92 x age (years)] + 5

WOMEN: BMR = [9.99 x weight (kg)] + [6.25 x height (cm)] - [4.92 x age (years)] -161

The above equation will give you your BMR – this is your Basal Metabolic Rate. In other words the number of calories your body needs to function while at rest.

You then multiply the BMR by an 'activity variable' to obtain your TDEE (total daily energy expenditure). This Activity Factor is the cost of living and it is based on more than just your workouts. It also includes work/lifestyle, sport & the thermogenic effect of food, (essentially the amount of energy burned in the process of digesting food).

 Average activity variables are as follows:

1.2 = Sedentary - Little or no exercise + desk job

1.3-1.4 = Lightly Active - Little daily activity & light exercise 1-3 days a week

1.5-1.6 = Moderately Active - Moderately active daily life & Moderate exercise 3-5 days a week

1.7-1.8 = Very Active - Physically demanding lifestyle & Hard exercise or sports 6-7 days a week

1.9-2.0 = Extremely Active - Hard daily exercise or sports and physical job

This number you have now calculated is the number of calories you need to consume to maintain your current weight.

If your goal is to lose weight, subtract 500 calories from this number and consume the specified amount of calories on a daily basis.

If your goal is to gain lean mass add 500 calories to this number and consume the specified amount of calories on a daily basis.

For a more in depth explanation of the principles and guidelines of Flexible Dieting and IIFYM consider reading the precursor to this book.

'Flexible Dieting 101: Eat the Foods you Love and Achieve the Body of Your Dreams'

Now that you have obtained your magic caloric number from the formula above let's step into the kitchen and create some great meals to help you reach your caloric goal!

Enter the Kitchen

From here on in you will find 160 of my favorite flexible dieting recipes, each recipe is categorized under a heading as to the most appropriate use or time to consume the particular meal.

Each recipe states the number of servings, as well as the calorie and macronutrient breakdown on a per serving basis.

Please note that these macronutrients and calories listed with each recipe are calculated using the exact ingredients in the recipe, If you wish to substitute ingredients bear in mind that this will adjust the macronutrient breakdown and calorie total of that meal.

Breakfast

Protein Pancakes

Oatmeal & Egg Whites

Light Breakfast

Scrambled Eggs with Spelt Flakes

Breakfast Fajitas

Big Breakfast Pizza

Vanilla Protein Porridge

Chocolate Peanut Butter & Banana Oatmeal

Apple Cinnamon Oatmeal

Peanut Butter, Banana Oat Breakfast Cookies

2 Minute Pancakes

French Toast Cups

Mocha Oatmeal

Banana Bread

Apple Crisp

Vanilla Cream Oatmeal

Chocolate Cookie Oatmeal

Protein Granola Yogurt

Blueberry Coconut Omelet

Banana Split Protein Oats

French Toast

Sausage and Egg Bell Pepper Breakfast

Stuffed Baked Breakfast Apple

Tomato Basil Omelet

Spicy Scrambled Eggs

Protein Pancakes

Serves: 6

Preparation time: 20 minutes

Cooking time: 15 minutes

Ingredients:

½ Banana mashed

½ cup (125ml) liquid Egg Whites

1 Tbsp. (15ml) Chia seeds

1 cup (250ml) organic quick Oats

1 scoop Peanut Butter flavored Whey Protein

½ cup (125ml) Almond Milk

½ cup (125ml) Water

Pinch of salt

Method:

Mix all the ingredients together in a large bowl, until well blended – you can use a hand mixer or blender for this as well.

Let the mixture sit for 10-15 minutes, allowing for the gluten to develop and the Chia seeds to expand, which will make your pancakes come out fluffier.

Heat a medium sized pan and coat with non-stick cooking spray.

Keep the heat on medium to thoroughly cook pancakes.

Use 1/3 cup (85ml) measuring cup and pour the mixture into the pan.

These pancakes take about 1½– 2 minutes on each side to cook.

Recommended Toppings:

Vanilla Greek Yogurt

Blueberries

Macronutrients: (per pancake)

Protein: 10g

Carbs: 12g

Fat: 2g

Calories: 66

Oatmeal & Egg Whites

Serves: 1

Preparation time: 5 minutes

Cooking time:5 minutes

Ingredients:

1½ oz (40g) Oatmeal

½ cup (125ml) Non-Fat Milk

1 tsp (5ml) Peanut Butter

1 tsp (5ml) 85% Dark Chocolate, chopped or grated

Pinch of Salt

On the side:

3 Egg Whites

½ slice of Non-Fat Cheese

Method:

Place the oats in a medium sized bowl, add the milk and cook it in the microwave on high for about 1½ minutes.

Add the peanut butter and chocolate, stir well.

Heat a frying pan over a medium heat and coat with a non-stick spray, add eggs and cook.

Place on a plate, add the cheese and mix for flavor

Macronutrients:

Protein: 25g

Carbs: 37g

Fat: 8g

Calories: 316

Light Breakfast

Serves: 1

Preparation time: 5 Minutes

Cooking time: none

Ingredients:

170g Chobani Greek Yogurt

2 heaped Tbsp (40ml) Jordan's Super Berry Granola

1 Banana chopped or mashed / alternatively ¼ cup (65ml) Blueberries

1 scoop Vanilla Whey Protein

Method:

Mix the whey powder and yogurt first, add the granola and banana and mix well.

Macronutrients:

Protein: 47g

Carbs: 10g

Fat: 2g

Calories 246

Scrambled Eggs with Spelt Flakes

Serves: 1

Preparation time: 5 Minutes

Cooking time: 5 Minutes

Ingredients:

2 whole Eggs

2 Egg Whites

20g Spelt Flakes

Chives, chopped

Pinch of Salt

Pepper to taste

Method:

Mix whole eggs and egg whites in a cup and flavor with salt and pepper to taste.

Heat a medium size frying pan and coat with nonstick spray.

Cook the eggs, and add the spelt flakes.

Garnish with chives and serve.

Macronutrients:

Protein: 34g

Carbs: 14g

Fats: 13g

Calories: 310

Breakfast Fajitas

Serves: 1

Preparation time: 5 minutes

Cooking time: 15 minutes

Ingredients:

6 Egg Whites

1 Egg Yolk

30g Fat-Free Cheddar Cheese, shredded

2 Fat-Free flour Tortillas

Salt to taste

Method:

Place the tortillas on a baking tray or plate.

Place eggs and yolk in a mixing bowl and beat well.

Heat the tortillas in either the microwave or oven.

Heat a skillet and coat with nonstick cooking spray. Cook the eggs over a medium flame, turn over and add the cheese.

Place eggs in tortillas and serve.

Additions:

Salsa

Parsley or chopped spring onion

Macronutrients:

Protein: 15g

Carbs: 16g

Fat: 0.5g

Calories:131

Big Breakfast Pizza

Servings: 1

Preparation time: 10 minutes

Cooking time: 10 minutes

Ingredients:

2 slices Jennie-O extra-lean Turkey Bacon. Alternatively, 1 turkey sausage patty

3 whole Eggs

¼ Boboli 12" thin Pizza Crust

½ cup (62ml) Fat-Free Mozzarella or Cheddar cheese

¼ small Onion, diced

½ Tomato, diced

Hot sauce (optional)

Salt and pepper to taste

Method:

If you are using turkey bacon, place bacon on a plate between two paper towels and microwave for one minute.

Flip bacon over, keeping it in the paper towels and remove the top paper towel. Place a new paper towel on top, and microwave for another minute.

Remove from microwave and cut into 1 inch pieces.

If making with turkey sausage, cook according to package instructions then cut into small pieces.

Place the pizza crust on a baking sheet and heat in a toaster oven.

Place the eggs in a mixing bowl, season with salt and pepper to taste, and beat well.

Heat a skillet and coat with a nonstick cooking spray. Sauté the onions and add the tomatoes. Add your choice of meat to the pan, and allow to simmer for a few minutes.

Add the beaten eggs and mix well. Add the hot sauce and remove from the heat.

Place the mixture on the heated pizza base and serve.

Tasty Additions:

Chopped spring onion

Chopped garlic

2 Chopped or sliced Mushrooms

Macronutrients:

Protein: 40g

Carbs: 49g

Fat: 22g

Calories: 575

Vanilla Protein Porridge

Servings: 1

Preparation time: 5 minutes

Cooking time: 2 minutes

Ingredients:

1 cup (250 ml) Oats

½ cup (125ml) Skim Milk

1 scoop Vanilla Protein whey (for variation, try other flavors)

½ tsp (2,5ml) Stevia or 1 Tbsp (15ml) Honey

Salt and Cinnamon to taste

Tasty Additions:

Mixed Berries or Blueberries

Method:

Place the oats, skim milk, stevia, salt, cinnamon and fruit in a microwave safe mixing bowl. Mix well and place in the microwave for 1 minute on high remove, stir and repeat. Remove and stir in the protein whey. Serve hot.

Macronutrients:

Protein: 45g

Carbs: 45g

Fat: 5g

Calories: 404

Chocolate Peanut Butter & Banana Oatmeal

Serves: 1

Preparation time: 5 Minutes

Cooking time: 2 Minutes

Ingredients:

1/2 cup (125ml) Oats

1/2 cup (125ml) Almond Milk

1 Banana, mashed

1 scoop Chocolate Peanut Butter Protein Powder

Pinch of Salt

Method:

Place the banana and milk in a mixing bowl and mix well.

Add the oats and mix.

Add ½ cup water, and mix.

Microwave for 2 minutes on high heat.

Remove and stir in the protein powder

Microwave for 1 more minute or longer for the consistency you like.

Macronutrients:

Protein: 33g

Carbs: 68g

Fat: 6g

Calories: 416

Apple Cinnamon Oatmeal

Serves: 1

Preparation time: 3 minutes

Cooking time: 3 minutes

Ingredients:

1 cup (250ml) rolled or steel cut Oats

½ cup (125ml) Water

½ an Apple, cut into small pieces

½ tsp (2,5ml) Cinnamon

1 scoop Vanilla Whey Protein

Pinch of Salt

Method:

Place the oats, apple, cinnamon, salt and water in a microwave safe mixing bowl, and mix well.

Microwave for 1 minutes on high heat, remove and stir then microwave for 1 more minute

Remove.

Mix in 1 scoop of vanilla whey protein.

Serve hot.

Macronutrients:

Protein: 30g

Carbs: 45g

Fat; 6g

Calories: 354

Peanut Butter, Banana Oat Breakfast Cookies

Servings: 16

Preparation time: 20 minutes

Cooking time: 30 minutes

Ingredients:

2 ripe Bananas, mashed until smooth & creamy

⅓ cup (85ml) Peanut Butter ~ creamy or chunky

⅔ cup (200ml) unsweetened Applesauce

1 scoop Vanilla Protein Powder

1 tsp (5ml) Vanilla Extract

1½ cups (375ml) Quick Cooking Oatmeal

¼ cup (63ml) chopped Nuts

Method:

Preheat heat oven to 350 F (180 C)

In a large bowl, mix mashed banana & peanut butter until completely combined then add in the applesauce, vanilla protein powder & the extract ~ mix again until all are completely combined.

Add in the oatmeal & nuts to the banana mixture & combine.

Let dough rest for 10 minutes.

Drop cookie dough, by spoonfuls, onto a parchment paper lined cookie sheet & flatten cookies into circles.

Bake cookies for 20-30 minutes, or until golden brown & done.

Macronutrients:

Protein: 4.5g

Carbs: 11.5g

Fat: 4.5g

Calories: 99

2 Minute Pancakes

Serves: 1

Preparation time: 5 minutes

Cooking time: 2 minutes

Ingredients:

4 Egg Whites.

1 scoop Chocolate Flavored Whey

45g Oats.

Method:

Mix in a bowl until you have a thick slurpy liquid.

Heat a skillet over a medium flame and Spray with a nonstick spray. Pour the mixture into the pan

Toppings

Yogurt

Fresh cut Fruit

Peanut Butter

Macronutrients:

Protein: 39g

Carbs: 35g

Fat: 3g

Calories: 323

French Toast Cups

Servings: 1

Preparation time: 5 minutes

Cooking time: 15 minutes

Ingredients:

2 eggs, or ½ cup (125ml) Egg Whites

1-2 tsp (10ml) Stevia

½ tsp (2,5ml) Vanilla Extract

¼ tsp (2ml) Cinnamon

Sea salt to taste

2 slices Wholegrain Bread

½ cup (125ml) Low-Fat Cottage Cheese

Method:

Preheat oven to 350 F (180 C).

In a shallow bowl, combine eggs, I tsp (5ml) Stevie, vanilla extract, a dash of cinnamon and salt, as desired. Dip bread slices into egg mixture, soaking thoroughly.

Spray 2 cups in a muffin tin with nonstick spray. Gently press one piece of bread into each cup. Press down to make sure they nearly touch the bottom of the pan.

Place muffin tin in oven and bake for 15 minutes.

In a separate bowl, mix the cottage cheese with remaining Stevia and cinnamon. Top each French toast cup with half of the mixture and serve hot.

Macronutrients:

Protein: 34g

Carbs: 28g

Fat:16g

Calories: 390

Mocha Oatmeal

Servings: 1

Preparation time: 5 minutes

Cooking time: 20 minutes

Ingredients:

1 cup (250ml) premade Instant Coffee

½ cup (125ml) Oatmeal

½ cup (125ml) Cottage Cheese

1 Tbsp. (15ml) unsweetened Cacao

½ cup (125ml) 1% Chocolate Milk

Method:

Cook oatmeal in the coffee for 15 minutes on the stovetop.

Add in the cottage cheese and the cacao and cook for another 5 minutes.

During the very last 2 minutes pour in the chocolate milk.

Add splenda or other sweetener if needed.

Macronutrients:

Protein: 27g

Carbs: 56g

Fat: 7g

Calories: 395

Banana Bread

Servings: 5

Preparation time: 10 minutes

Cooking time: 35 minutes

Ingredients:

1 cup (250ml) Oatmeal

2 small Bananas, mashed

1 Egg

½ cup (125 ml) Skim Milk

2 tsp (10ml) Cinnamon

100g Low Fat Cottage Cheese

1 heaped scoop of Banana or Vanilla Flavored Whey Protein (about 40 grams)

1 tsp (5ml) Baking Powder

Method:

Preheat the oven to 350 F (180 C).

Spray a small bread-loaf tin with a nonstick spray.

Mix all the ingredients together, and pour into a baking tin.

Bake for 35 minutes until golden brown.

Serve cooled.

Macronutrients (per serving):

Protein: 13g

Carbs: 23g

Fat: 4g

Calories: 191

Apple Crisp

Servings: 1

Preparation time: 10 minutes

Cooking time: None

Ingredients:

½ cup (125ml) rolled Oats

1 cup (250ml) Kashi GoLean cereal

10-15 Raisins

1 Tbsp (15ml) Honey

½ Tbsp (7,5ml) Cinnamon or to taste

1 small Granny Smith or Golden Delicious Apple, diced finely

150ml Water

Method:

Place everything in a mixing bowl and mix before adding the water (a little more if you want) Mix well and consume immediately.

Macronutrients:

Protein: 19g

Carbs: 92g

Fat: 4g

Calories: 420

Vanilla Cream Oatmeal

Servings: 1

Preparation time: 7 minutes

Cooking time: 2 minutes

Ingredients:

1 cup (250ml) Oatmeal

1cup (250ml) Skim Milk

1 scoop (30g) Vanilla Protein Powder

½ tsp (2,5ml) of Stevia

Pinch of Cinnamon

Pinch of Salt

Method:

In a microwave proof mixing bowl, add the salt, oatmeal skim milk and cinnamon, mix well. Place in the microwave and cook at full power for about 1 minute - stir the mix , then microwave for another 1 minute period.

Let the oatmeal cool for about 3 minutes add the Stevia and protein powder.

Consume immediately.

Macronutrients:

Protein: 45g

Carbs: 73g

Fat: 6g

Calories: 531

Chocolate Cookie Oatmeal

Servings: 1

Preparation time: 5 minutes

Cooking time: None

Ingredients:

½ cup (125ml) uncooked Oats

1 Tbsp (15ml) natural Peanut Butter

1 scoop (40g) Chocolate Whey Powder

4 Tbsp (60ml) boiling Water

2 packets Splenda

Method:

Add water to oats, and let it stand for 30 seconds.

Add whey, splenda and peanut butter, and mix well.

Consume immediately.

Macronutrients:

Protein: 31g

Carbs: 32g

Fat: 12g

Calories: 370

Protein Granola Yogurt

Servings: 1

Preparation time: 20 minutes

Cooking time: None

Ingredients:

¾ cup (180ml) Fat Free Greek Yogurt

1 Scoop (30g) Vanilla Protein Powder

1 Tbsp (15ml) Chia Seeds

2 Tbsp (30ml) Granola/Granola Type Cereal

⅔ cup (100g) chopped Strawberries

Alternative fruits:

Blueberries

Cranberries

Apple

Method:

Place all the ingredients except the fruit in a small mixing or serving bowl and mix well. Allow to stand for 15-20 minutes, to allow the chia seeds to swell and the granola to soften.

Add the fruit, mix and enjoy.

Tips:

This yogurt can be frozen, and consumed as a filling treat on a warm day.

Macronutrients:

Protein: 46g

Carbs: 52g

Fat: 5g

Calories: 437

Blueberry Coconut Omelet

Serves: 1

Preparation time: 10 minutes

Cooking time: 5 minutes

Ingredients:

1 tsp (5ml) Coconut Oil

½ cup (125ml) liquid Egg Whites

¼ tsp (2ml) Vanilla Extract

Pinch of Salt

½ tsp (2,5ml) Sweetener or Stevia

⅓ cup (85ml) thawed or fresh Blueberries

1 Tbsp (15ml) desiccated or shredded Coconut

½ Tbsp (7,5ml) White Chocolate Peanut Butter

Method:

Combine the egg whites, salt, vanilla & sweetener/cinnamon in a small mixing bowl and mix. Well

Heat a small frying pan over medium heat and add the coconut oil.

Once the pan is hot, pour in the mixture. As the mixture starts to set add your blueberries & coconut to one half, and cook for another minute or so, before flipping.

Cook for another minute, flip the omelet one last time onto its other side, and cook until golden brown and add the peanut butter to the top of the omelet.

Fold the omelet and serve immediately.

Nutrition Facts:

Protein: 15g

Carbs: 13g

Fat: 11g

Calories: 208

Banana Split Protein Oats

Serves: 1

Preparation time: Overnight

Cooking time: None

Ingredients:

1 cup (250ml) Blue Diamond Almond Breeze Unsweetened Vanilla Milk

1 scoop (30g) BSN Syntha-6 Peanut Butter Protein Powder

1 small Banana

½ cup (125ml) dry Quaker Old Fashioned Oats

¼ cup Almond Milk

4 tsp (20ml) Walden Farms Sugar Free Calorie Free Chocolate Syrup

2 packets Stevia Sweetener

Chopped Nuts, (optional)

Method:

In a small mixing bowl combine the oats, Sythna, peanut butter cookie protein powder, stevia, and almond milk, and allow to swell overnight

The following morning, cut the banana in half lengthwise, and place in a dish.

Put the oat mix in between the banana halves

Top with Walden Farms Chocolate Syrup, and chopped nuts.

Macronutrients:

Protein: 30g

Carbs: 64g

Fat: 12g

Calories: 470

French Toast

Serves: 3

Preparation time: 5 minutes

Cooking time: 5 minutes

Ingredients:

6 slices Sara lee Delightful Whole Wheat and Honey 45 calorie bread

250g Egg Whites

½ cup (125ml) unsweetened Almond Milk

2 packets sweetener or Stevia

½ tsp (2ml) Baking Powder/Baking Soda

Method:

Preheat a pancake griddle at a medium heat

Combine the egg whites, almond milk, baking powder, and sweetener in a shallow dish

Using two forks, place each slice of bread in the egg mixture, turning over to saturate both sides.

Place each slice on the griddle and cook until a golden color is achieved, turn and repeat.

Top with your favorite syrup or jam, but remember to adjust the macros!

Tips:

Use a medium high heat if you desire a more moist toast, as the outside will be done prior to drying out the inside.

Also for a more moist toast, decrease the amount of egg whites and/or increase the amount of almond milk. Vice versa for a crispier toast. The amount of necessary egg whites may vary by the bread you use. The Sara Lee bread absorbs liquid like a sponge!

Macronutrients (per serving):

Protein: 46g

Carbs: 43

Fat: 4g

Calories: 423

Sausage and Egg Bell Pepper Breakfast

Serves: 1

Preparation time: 15 minutes

Cooking time: 10 minutes

Ingredients:

1 medium Publix Red Bell Pepper

2 large Egg Whites

½ cup (125ml) cooked Turkey Breakfast Sausage

2 Tbsp (10g) Cheddar or American Cheese (Reduced Fat, Pasteurized)

⅔ tsp (4ml) Parsley

Method:

Preheat the oven to 400 F (220 C)

Prepare 90% lean turkey breakfast sausage in advance.

Cut the top off a bell pepper and place into an oven (directly on the rack) at for 10 minutes.

Scramble 2 egg whites in a pan. Combine with your prepared turkey sausage. Mix in the shredded reduced fat cheddar cheese. Stuff into finished bell pepper and top with parsley or green onions.

Macronutrients:

Protein: 27g

Carbs: 9g

Fat: 7g

Calories: 212

Stuffed Baked Breakfast Apple

Serves: 3

Preparation time: 10 minutes

Cooking time: 10 minutes

Ingredients:

3 Granny Smith of Golden Delicious Apples, cored and pitted

1½ cups (375ml) Non-fat Greek Yogurt

1 scoop (30g) Vanilla Protein Powder

½ cup (125ml) rolled Oats

3 Tbsp (45ml) chopped Walnuts

1 tsp (5ml) Cinnamon

2 Tbsp (30ml) Splenda Brown Sugar Blend

Method:

Combine the cinnamon and brown sugar.

Place the cored apple in the mixture. Coat the apple, inside and out, and place on the grill.

Cook for 3-4 minutes or until tender.

Mix the Greek yogurt, protein powder, rolled oats, and walnuts until well mixed.

Fill the baked apple with the mixture.

Cover and cook for 1-2 minutes or until yogurt is heated.

Macronutrients:

Protein:25 g

Carbs: 50g

Fat: 11g

Calories: 393

Tomato Basil Omelet

Serves: 1

Preparation time: 5 minutes

Cooking time: 5 minutes

Ingredients:

3 free range Eggs

10 Cherry Tomatoes

Fresh Basil

Sea Salt

Black Pepper

Kelp

1 Tbsp (15ml) Palm Oil, for cooking

Method:

In a mixing bowl, whisk 3 whole eggs with salt, pepper, basil, and kelp.

Slice 10 cherry tomatoes.

Coat skillet with palm oil.

Pour everything into the skillet and cook over medium heat.

If you add sausage, brown it in a separate pan before adding it to the omelet.

Flip once. When done fold and serve immediately.

Macronutrients:

Protein: 10g

Carbs: 12g

Fat: 11g

Calories: 186

Spicy Scrambled Eggs

Serves: 1

Preparation time: 5 minutes

Cooking time: 5 minutes

Ingredients:

2 large Whole Eggs

4 Eggs Whites

¼ of an Onion, finely chopped

1 whole red Chili (or chili to taste), finely chopped

1 clove Garlic, finely chopped

50g Cottage Cheese

Pinch of Mixed Herbs

2 slices of whole Brown Bread

Method:

In a small mixing bowl combine the whole eggs and egg whites. Whisk until the egg yolks and whites mix.

To this, add the chopped onion, garlic and chili, mix well.

Finally, add the cottage cheese and a pinch of mixed herbs, Whisk.

Heat a small non-stick frying pan over a medium flame, coat with a non-stick spray.

Empty the contents of the mixing bowl into the frying pan.

Put your toast in the toaster. Gently stir the contents to scramble the eggs

Once eggs are scrambled, add them to toast on a large plate.

Macronutrients:

Protein: 50g

Carbs: 34g

Fat: 19g

Calories: 507

Main Meals

Thai Spiced Chicken Beef and Basil

High Protein BBQ Chicken Pizza

Turkey Chili Frito Pie

Flavorsome Chicken Stir fry

Egg 'n Tuna

Tortilla Pizza

High Protein Sandwiches

Asian Wok

No-nonsense Chicken Noodles

Chicken Pad Thai

Steamed Hamburgers with Sweet Potato Fries

Spicy Pasta

Butternut Lasagne

Chilli Con Turkey

Turkey Burgers

Chicken Cordon Bleu

Lean Turkey Meatloaf

Salsa Chicken Tortilla

Bistro-Style White Bean Burger with Fried Egg and Avocado

Couscous Salad with Tuna and Avocado

Herb Garden Beef Burger

Beef and Rice Mash

Avocado Lime Chicken

Marinated Chicken Enchiladas

Spanish Rice

Asian Flank Steak and Stir-Fry

Protein Pumpkin Pie

Baked Chicken

Turkey Power Balls

Honey Nut Barbeque Chicken Fingers

Chicken Egg White Pizza

Curry Rice

Salmon Balls

Peanut Butter Chicken

Baked Pineapple Chicken

Slow Cooked Chicken Stew

Italian Slow Cooked Chicken

Sloppy Joes

Creamy Artichoke Chicken

Spicy Coconut Chicken Tenders

Peanut Butter Chicken

Chicken Avocado Burger Patties

Tuna Melt

Chicken Pot Pie

Spicy Chicken Lentils

Spicy Turkey Chili

Rotisserie Chicken Noodle Pasta Bake

Teriyaki Salmon

Field of Greens

Lobster Boat

Spicy Turkey Meatballs

Chicken Cheese Meatballs

Chicken Caesar Meatballs

Fish in Foil

Chicken Cucumber Salad

Sweet Potato Omelet

Thai Spicy Beef Salad

Malaysian Curry Prawns

Chicken Curry

Beef Chop Suey

Salsa Quinoa Chicken

Grilled Tuna Burgers

Tuna Cheese Melt

Beef and Basil

Serves: 1

Preparation time: 5 minutes

Cooking time: 5 minutes

Ingredients:

Spinach

Corn

Baby Tomatoes

Mushrooms

Minced Fresh Basil

Eggs

Lean Sirloin Steak (150g - 200g)

Method:

Begin by boiling 1 egg.

Warm a pan with some olive oil. Thrown in handful of corn and halved baby tomatoes.

Stir fry for a little, and add some minced basil.

Add your sliced mushrooms.

Prep your salad bowl with spinach as the base.

Once the corn, tomato and mushroom mixture is basiled up

Heat a little oil in a pan and place the sirloin steak in. A little of salt and pepper on the uncooked side is enough for seasoning.

After a couple of minutes, flip the meat.

Place the meat on a plate and rest for a further 3-5minutes to ensure the juices redistribute throughout the meat. Peel the egg and mash up in a small bowl.

Place a mound of the spinach, corn,tomato and mushroom salad on a plate.

Place thin slices of the sirloin on top

Grab the egg mixture and place a thin strip of it on top of the steak.

Macronutrients: (per serve)

Protein: 57 Grams

Carbs: 23 Grams

Fat: 15 Grams

Calories: 463

High Protein BBQ Chicken Pizza

Serves: 8

Preparation time: 10 minutes

Cooking time: 20 minutes

Ingredients:

1 Whole Boboli Whole Wheat Thin Pizza Crust

3 servings (90g) 2% Mozzarella shredded cheese

13oz (850g) boneless Chicken Breast

½ Tbsp (7,5ml) Olive Oil

2.5oz (74ml) chopped Onions

2 servings (60ml) BBQ Sauce

Method:

Preheat a skillet on a medium-high flame, and your oven to 450 F (220 C)

Chop chicken and onions

Pour olive oil in preheated skillet

Place chicken and onions in skillet, stir so olive oil coats the chicken/onions. Season and cook thoroughly

Open Boboli pizza crust and baste with BBQ sauce

Place the cooked chicken on pizza crust and cover with cheese

Cook in oven for 12 minutes

Macronutrients: (per serve)

Protein: 20g

Carbs: 20g

Fat: 5g

Calories: 210

Turkey Chili Frito Pie

Serves: 1

Preparation time: 5 minutes

Cooking time: 5 minutes

Ingredients:

1 can Wolf Brand Turkey Chili.

60g 2% Milk Shredded Cheese

30g of plain Fritos

Method:

Empty the contents of the tin into a microwave proof bowl.

Place in microwave and cook at full power for a minute and a half.

Remove the bowl and stir well.

Sprinkle the cheese on top and return to the microwave for a minute,

Add 1 serving of plain Fritos and stir.

Serve immediately.

Macronutrients:

Protein: 71g

Carbs: 47.5g

Fats 33g

Calories: 771

Flavorsome Chicken Stir fry

Serves: 1

Preparation time: 5 minutes

Cooking time: 35 minutes

Ingredients:

150g Chicken, cut in strips

100g Broccoli broken up

2 slices of Pineapple cut into chunks

1 tsp (5ml) Soy Sauce

1 tsp (5ml) Olive Oil

100g uncooked Brown rice

Method:

Boil the brown rice.

Heat a wok and add a small amount of water with the olive oil.

Place the broccoli in the middle and cook for 5 minutes.

Move the broccoli to the outsides and add the chicken, and fry for 2 minutes.

Mix the broccoli and chicken then add the pineapple and soy sauce, and cook for 2 minutes.

Add the cooked rice to the wok and mix.

Add seasoning (hot sauce), if desired

Macronutrients:

Protein: 47g

Carbs: 70g

Fats: 14g

Calories: 585

Egg 'n Tuna

Serves: 1

Preparation time: 5 minutes

Cooking time: 5 minutes

Ingredients:

135g (1 can) Tuna,

2 Whole Eggs

100g of Cottage Cheese

20g of Cheese

Method:

Heat a small frying pan, and coat it with a nonstick spray.

Open and drain the tuna, and add to the pan, cook for two minutes.

Add the cottage cheese, and mix well.

Add salt and pepper to taste.

Shell the two eggs and beat lightly, then add to the mixture.

Cook until eggs are done.

Add the cheese and cheese, and serve immediately.

Macronutrients:

Protein: 66g

Carbs: 2g

Fats: 19g

Calories: 443

Tortilla Pizza

Serves: 1

Preparation time: 5 minutes

Cooking time: 10 minutes

Ingredients:

1 Plain tortilla

40g Low-Fat Mozzarella

⅓ jar Napolina Pizza Sauce

200g Chicken Breast, cut in strips or cubes

Method:

Heat a small skillet and spray with nonstick spray,

Cook the chicken, add seasoning if desired.

Lay tortilla flat and spread the pizza sauce over it, and sprinkle with the cheese.

Add the chicken and place under the grill until the cheese has melted.

Serve immediately

Macronutrients:

Protein: 62g

Carbs: 40g

Fats: 12g

Calories: 516

High Protein Sandwiches

Serves: 1

Preparation time: 5 minutes

Cooking time: 5 minutes

Ingredients:

5 large Egg Whites

2 Bread

1 Tbsp (15ml) Olive oil

4 Tbsp 60ml Cheddar cheese

Salt and Pepper to taste

Method:

Heat a medium sized skillet over a low-medium flame and add the olive oil.

Add the egg whites into the pan and cook for two minutes or until whites have set.

Sprinkle the cheddar cheese onto egg, and allow to melt.

Season with salt and pepper.

Fold the egg first in half then in quarters and place in a slice of bread

Season with sauce if so desired

Cover with another slice and serve immediately.

Macronutrients:

Protein: 30g

Carbs: 31g

Fats: 7g

Calories: 307

Asian Wok

Serves: 1

Preparation time: 10 minutes

Cooking time: 30 minutes

Ingredients:

150g Chicken cut into strips

100g Basmati rice

50g Zucchini grated

½ tsp (2.5ml) Paprika

2 tsp (10ml) Wok sauce

Curry Powder

Method:

Boil the rice according to cooking directions.

Heat a wok and add a small amount of water with the olive oil.

Place the Zucchini in the middle and cook for 2 minutes.

Move the Zucchini to the outsides and add the chicken, and fry for 5 minutes.

Mix the Zucchini and chicken then add the paprika, curry powder and wok sauce, and cook for 2 minutes.

Add the cooked rice to the wok and mix.

Add seasoning (hot sauce), if desired.

Macronutrients:

Protein: 43g

Carbs: 84g

Fats: 4g

Calories: 528

No-nonsense Chicken Noodles

Serves: 1

Preparation time: 5 minutes

Cooking time: 5 minutes

Ingredients:

100g egg noodles

250g chicken breast cut in strips

Chili sauce to taste

Worcester sauce to taste

Tikka powder to taste

Method:

Boil 100g egg noodles,

Heat a medium sized frying pan once a medium high flame and coat with nonstick spray.

Add chicken and cook,

When chicken is almost cooked, add chili sauce, Worcester sauce and tikka powder, lower the heat and allow to simmer.

Brain the noodles and place in a bowl, season with Worcester sauce if desired.

Place chicken on noodles.

Serve immediately

Macronutrients:

Protein: 80g

Carbs: 60g

Fats: 10g

Calories: 540

Chicken Pad Thai

Serves: 1

Preparation time: 5 minutes

Cooking time: 10 minutes

Ingredients:

2 cups (500ml) cooked Whole Wheat Angel Hair Pasta

3.3oz. (95g) Chicken Breasts, cut into bite sized pieces

1 cup (250ml) sliced Mushrooms

½ cup (125l) sliced Yellow Pepper

1 Tbsp (15ml) Fish Sauce

¼ cup (63ml)chopped cilantro

1 tsp (5ml) olive oil

1 Tbsp (15ml)natural peanut butter

1 Tbsp. (15ml) Splenda (3packets)

1 Tbsp. red Chili Flakes

Method:

Prepare the pasta according to package directions.

Heat the oil in a skillet over medium heat, and add the chicken, cook for 2-3 minutes.

Add the peppers and mushrooms and cook for another 3-5 minutes or until chicken is fully cooked.

Mix the fish sauce, peanut butter, Splenda, and chili flakes and pour over the chicken.

Cover, and simmer for 3-4 minutes.

Top with cilantro before serving.

Macronutrients:

Protein: 56g

Carbs: 39g

Fat: 14g

Calories: 458

Steamed Hamburgers with Sweet Potato Fries

Serves: 1

Preparation time: 10 minutes

Cooking time: 25 minutes

Ingredients:

1 Chicken Filet (about 150-200 grams)

2 Whole Wheat Hamburger Buns

Lettuce, Cucumber, Tomato, Onion as garnish

2 Sweet Potatoes

1 tsp (5ml) Olive Oil

Salt, Pepper, Basil

1 big Tomato

Method:

Preheat the oven to 450 F (230 C).

Put the chicken fillet through the meat grinder and season it.

Cut French fries of your sweet potatoes, add one teaspoon of olive oil and season it with a pinch of salt, pepper and garlic.

Divide the chicken and place the meat in empty tuna cans and place in a steamer. Set a timer for about 15-20 minutes.

Insert potatoes in the oven. After 10-15 minutes, turn the fries so they can become crispy on both sides.

Garnish the hamburger buns with some lettuce, tomato, cucumber, onion.

Finish it off with the hamburgers and some dressing of your choice.

Macronutrients:

Proteins: 56g

Carbs: 152g

Fats: 5g

Calories: 806

Spicy Pasta

Serves: 1

Preparation time: 5 minutes

Cooking time: 15 minutes

Ingredients:

2 Trader Joe's Spicy Italian Chicken Sausages

4 oz (120g) Ground Beef

4oz (120g) boneless, skinless Chicken Breast

1 cup (250ml) Whole Wheat Penne

Fresh Basil

Garlic, chopped or crushed

2 Tbsp (15ml) EVOO

2 Tomatoes, chopped

Method:

Cook paste as per package instructions.

Heat a medium sized frying pan and add the beef chicken tomatoes and cook them together. Add the sausages, and allow to simmer over a low hat for 5-10 minutes.

Add some freshly chopped garlic and basil, and cook until basil has wilted.

Drain pasta and place on plate, spoon the meat over and garnish with EVVO.

Serve immediately.

Macronutrients:

Protein: 103g

Carbs: 126g

Fat: 59g

Calories: 1,430

Butternut Lasagna

Serves: 4

Preparation time: 20 minutes

Cooking time: 95 minutes

Ingredients:

1½ lbs (620g) Butternut Squash, cut and deseeded

3.5 oz (100g) Lasagna Noodles (sheets)

500g Cottage or Ricotta Cheese

5 cups (1.25ℓ) Spinach, chopped

50g shredded Cheese

Sauce:

2 cups (500ml) Milk

3 Tbsp (45ml) Flour

Method:

Cook the butternut squash:

Preheat oven to 450 F (230 C).

Split butternut in half. Place in baking dish and fill about 1inch (2,5cm) of water. Place in oven and bake for 40 minutes, until tender. Scoop out flesh and discard skin, mash the flesh.

Adjust oven to 350 F (180 C)

Filling: Wilt spinach in a pan, then cool and add 500g cottage cheese and stir.

Sauce: Heat up milk in small saucepan on low heat. Whisk in small amounts of flour; roughly ½ teaspoon at a time. Once all flour has been mixed in, bring up to a boil, whisking continuously. Once the sauce thickens, turn heat off (use immediately).

Once the squash, filling, and sauce are finished, you are ready to start building your dish.

Use cooking spray or a light swipe of cooking oil to cover a 9 x 13 cooking dish. Use 1 cup of the sauce to cover the entire bottom of the dish. Place a layer of (cooked or uncooked) noodles side by side to make the next layer of the lasagna, use half of the ricotta/cottage cheese and spinach mixture to cover the noodles.

Next, layer all of the roasted butternut squash, followed by the last half of the ricotta/cottage cheese spinach filling. Top with another layer of lasagna noodles, then cover those with the remaining sauce and the grated cheese.

Cover the Butternut Squash Lasagna with tin foil and bake at for 40 minutes. Uncover and cook for another 15 minutes. Let it cool for 5 minutes before serving.

Macronutrients (per serve):

Protein: 101g

Carb: 201g

Fat: 30g

Calories: 1,470

Chili Con Turkey

Serves: 4

Preparation time: 5 minutes

Cooking time: 5 minutes

Ingredients:

450g ground Turkey

1 can Mexican style diced Tomatoes

1 can Black Beans, rinsed and drained

1 can whole-kernel Sweet Corn, drained

1 package dried Chili mix

1 Tbsp (15ml) Ground Flaxseed

1/4 cup (63ml) Water

1 cup (250ml) cooked Rice

Method:

Brown the turkey in a skillet over medium high heat

Add everything else but the rice and cook over low heat for 10 minutes.

Serve over rice

Macronutrients (per serve):

Protein: 30g

Carbs: 52g

Fats: 11g

Calories: 407

Turkey Burgers

Serves: 1

Preparation time: 10 minutes

Cooking time: 30 minutes

Ingredients:

125g of Turkey Breast mince

¼ cup (63ml) of finely diced Onion

¼ cup (63ml) of finely diced Red Pepper

1 Garlic clove, peeled and minced

¼ tsp (1ml) ground Black Pepper

2 tsp (10ml) of Olive Oil

Method:

Preheat your oven to 350 F (180 C)

Add the diced red pepper, diced onion, minced garlic, turkey breast mince to a mixing bowl. Add the olive oil and the ground black pepper. Mix well and add any spices if you would like to enhance the flavor.

Form two patties and place on the grill.

Cook the patties in the oven for13 minutes. Then turn over and cook for another 13 minutes.

Serve with whole-meal teacakes, lettuce, tomato and onion.

Macronutrients:

Protein: 39.5 g

Carbs: 13.3 g

Fats: 2.6 g

Calories: 175.8

Chicken Cordon Bleu

Serves: 2

Preparation time: 10 minutes

Cooking time: 30 minutes

Ingredients:

4oz (120g) boneless skinless Chicken Breasts

8 Kirkland Honey Smoked Ham slices

½ cup (125ml) Reduced-Fat shredded Mozzarella

Salt, Pepper and Garlic seasoning to taste

1 cup (250ml)-mashed Sweet Potato

6 oz (170g) Kirkland stir-fry frozen vegetables

4 Ritz Crackers, crushed.

Method:

Pre-heat oven to 375 F (200 C)

Pound the chicken breast to ¼ inch (6mm) thickness.

Season both sides with salt, pepper, garlic powder, place 2 slices of ham on top of breasts, Sprinkle with shredded mozzarella and roll up,

Sprinkle the top of the rolls with crushed ritz crackers.

Bake in oven for 25-30 minutes at 375.

Wash and peel sweet potatoes. Cube the potatoes and steam boil potatoes for about 25 minutes.

Place 6 oz of frozen veggies in small saucepan, boil with ¼ cup water and season to taste.

Macronutrients (per serve):

Protein: 38g

Carbs: 60g

Fats: 12g

Calories: 443

Lean Turkey Meatloaf

Serves: 2

Preparation time: 10 minutes

Cooking time: 50 minutes

Ingredients:

1lb (450g) of Ground Turkey

½ can of Tomato Sauce

2 whole Eggs

1 cup (250ml) of Whole-Wheat Breadcrumbs

½ Onion, diced.

Seasoning and Salt to your taste.

Method:

Preheat oven to 375 F (180 C)

Mix all ingredients together in a bowl, place the mixture in a baking tray lined with foil, shape into a loaf, bake for 45 minutes.

Top with shrircha hot sauce and a little BBQ sauce, then place in oven for another 15 minutes

Macronutrients:

Protein: 28g

Carbs: 18g

Fats: 4g

Calories: 220

Salsa Chicken Tortilla

Serves: 1

Preparation time: 5 minutes

Cooking time: 10 minutes

Ingredients:

¾ cup (190 ml) diced precooked Chicken

2 Tbsp (30ml) diced Onion

2 Tbsp (30ml) Feta-Cheese crumbles

1 handful romaine lettuce, chopped

1 large whole-wheat tortilla

Salsa for dipping

Method:

Arrange the chicken, onion, cheese, and lettuce down the center of the tortilla.

Roll it tightly and cut it in half.

Grill the rolls seam-side down for 2 to 3 minutes per side, on a nonstick skillet heated to medium.

Serve with salsa. Makes 1 serving

Macronutrients:

Protein: 56g

Carbs: 10g

Fats: 10g

Calories: 397

Bistro-Style White Bean Burger with Fried Egg and Avocado

Serves: 1

Preparation time: 5 minutes

Cooking time: 20 minutes

Ingredients:

1 cup (250ml) white Kidney Beans, drained and mashed

8oz (230g) Portobello mushrooms, grilled and finely chopped

½ cup (125ml) Spelt flakes

½ cup (125ml) marinated Artichoke Hearts, chopped and patted dry

2 Tbsp (30ml) sun-dried Tomatoes, finely chopped

1 tsp (5ml) balsamic vinegar

4 cups (1ℓ) Mixed Greens

Garnish

4 eggs, fried sunny side up

½ Avocado, sliced

¼ tsp (1ml) sea salt and pepper

Method:

Preheat oven to 400 F (200 C)

Line a baking sheet with parchment paper and set aside.

Using clean hands, combine the first 6 ingredients and form into 4 equal-sized patties. Place onto lined baking sheet and bake for 20-minutes.

Divide greens equally between 4 plates. Remove patties from oven and place over the bed of greens. Garnish each burger with a fried egg (if desired). Divide avocado slices evenly between burgers and sprinkle each evenly with sea salt and pepper.

Macronutrients:

Protein: 14g

Carbs: 24 g

Fats: 3g

Calories: 281

Couscous Salad with Tuna and Avocado

Serves: 1

Preparation time: 10 minutes

Cooking time: 30 minutes

Ingredients:

70g Couscous

125g Kidney Beans

250g Cherry Tomatoes

150g Spinach

1 Pepper

60g of light Feta

150g Tuna

½ Onion

100g Avocado

Method:

Cook the Couscous and let it cool.

Combine everything except avocado and feta and mix thoroughly.

Top with avocado and feta.

Season with lemon pepper/garlic/fresh lemon/balsamic

Macronutrients:

Protein: 76g

Carbs: 97g

Fat: 24g

Calories: 884

Herb Garden Beef Burger

Serves: 4

Preparation time: 10 minutes

Cooking time: 15 minutes

Ingredients:

1 cup (250ml) chopped fresh Herb Mix (dill, basil, parsley, mint and rosemary), divided

1lb (450g) extra-lean Ground Beef

2 tsp (10ml) ground Cumin

¼ tsp (1ml) each Sea Salt and Pepper

Sauce

½ cup (125ml) Low-Fat plain Greek yogurt

1 tsp (5ml) minced/crushed Garlic

½ tsp (2,5ml) Lime Zest

Method:

Measure out 2 Tbsp (30ml) of herb mixture and set aside.

Using clean hands, combine remaining herbs, beef, cumin, salt and pepper, and form into 4-equal sized patties.

Grill at med-high heat for 5 to 7 minutes per side, or until cooked as desired.

Stir together reserved 2 Tbsp of herbs (30ml), yogurt, garlic and lime zest. Divide yogurt mixture evenly between burgers.

Macronutrients (per burger):

Protein: 32g

Carbs: 3g

Fat: 10g

Calories: 234

Beef and Rice Mash

Serves: 2

Preparation time: 5 minutes

Cooking time: 5 minutes

Ingredients:

16oz (450g) lean, Ground Beef

1 cup (250ml) cooked Rice

1 Swanson Beef flavor pack

1 Tbsp (15ml) dry Parsley

2 Tbsp (30ml) Fat Free Chicken Broth (in the box)

¼ cup (63ml) Water

1 Tbsp (15ml) Garlic Powder

Season-All to taste (about 2 Tbsp)

Method:

Put the ground beef (mince) in a deeper non-stick pan with a lid and add season-all, garlic powder, and dry parsley and begin to brown on medium heat. As soon as meat begins to brown, stir and then add the cooked rice, flavor packet, water, and broth. Cover and allow to simmer for 15 minutes, stirring 3-4 times.

Macronutrients (per serve):

Protein: 96g

Carbs: 246g

Fat: 32g

Calories: 894

Avocado Lime Chicken

Serves: 1

Preparation time: 5 minutes

Cooking time: 5 minutes

Ingredients:

¼ cup (63ml) Brown Rice

6 oz. (170g) grilled Chicken

½ Lime

1 Avocado

¼-½ packet Stevia

Method:

Grill the chicken breast.

Boil/steam the brown rice.

Cut the Avocado into small cubes while the chicken and rice cooks.

Squeeze the juice from the lime and add 1/4-1/2 packet of stevia.

Place the rice, chicken, and avocado into a bowl/tupperware. Pour the lime juice on top. Mix it all together. You can add cilantro or whatever you want to it after that.

Macronutrients:

Protein: 54g

Carbs: 45 g

Fat: 37g

Calories: 726

Marinated Chicken Enchiladas

Servings: 6

Preparation time: 15 minutes

Cooking time: 35 minutes

Basting time: Overnight

Ingredients:

1lb. (450g) boneless, skinless Chicken Breasts, cut into cubes

1 tsp (5ml) Olive Oil

Juice of 1 Lime

1 tsp (5ml) Chili Powder

2 Scallions, minced

Salt and Pepper to taste

1 (15-oz.) can Black Beans, drained and rinsed

6 (6-inch/15cm) Whole-Wheat Tortillas

2/3 cup (180ml) Reduced-Fat shredded Mexican cheese blend or Monterey Jack cheese, divided

1½ cups (375ml) canned Enchilada Sauce

Method:

In a medium bowl, combine the chicken with the olive oil, lime juice, chili powder, scallions, salt, and pepper.

Cover and marinate in the refrigerator for at least 1 hour and up to 24 hours.

Preheat the oven to 375°F (190°C)

Remove the chicken from the marinade and discard the excess.

Heat the olive oil in a nonstick skillet over medium heat. Add the chicken and sauté for 7 to 8 minutes until chicken is cooked through. Remove the chicken to a bowl and add the black beans.

Divide the chicken-and-bean filling among six tortillas. Top each with 1 Tbsp. of the cheese. Roll up each tortilla and place seam-side down in a baking dish coated with cooking spray. Pour the sauce over the enchiladas and bake, covered, for about 20 minutes.

Add the remaining cheese and bake, uncovered, for 5 minutes until cheese melts.

Macronutrients (per serve):

Protein: 26g

Carbs: 30g

Fat:9g

Calories 305

Spanish Rice

Serves: 8

Preparation time: 10 minutes

Cooking time: 30 minutes

Ingredients:

1lb (450g) lean Ground Turkey

1-15oz can Tomato Sauce

1-14.5oz can Diced Tomatoes

1 11oz Diced Tomatoes with Chili Peppers

2 cups (500ml) uncooked instant Brown Rice

1 cup (250ml) Water

2½ tsp (12,5ml) Chili Powder

2 tsp Worcestershire sauce

Method:

Brown turkey in skillet, drain off fat and discard.

Return drained turkey to skillet. Add tomato sauce, tomatoes, rice water, chili powder and Worcestershire sauce. Stir to mix ingredients. Cover and simmer 20 to 25 minutes. Stir before serving.

Macronutrients (per serve):

Protein: 18g

Carbs: 44g

Fat:7g

Calories 310

Asian Flank Steak and Stir-Fry

Serves: 6

Preparation time: 30 minutes

Cooking time: 20 minutes

Ingredients:

4 Tbsp (60ml) Light Soy Sauce, divided

1 Tbsp (15ml) Rice Vinegar

1½ Tbsp (22.5ml) Arrowroot or Cornstarch, divided

1lb (450g) flank Steak, trimmed of all fat

¾ cup (180ml) Low-Fat, reduced-sodium Beef or Bhicken Broth, divided

4 Tbsp (20ml) Hoisin Sauce

1 tsp (5ml) Chili Puree with Garlic

1 Tbsp (15ml) Canola Oil, divided

3 cloves Garlic, minced

1 Tbsp (15ml) minced Ginger

2 stalks Celery, sliced

2 cups (500ml) sliced Broccoli

1 medium Red Pepper, cut into strips

1½ (375ml) cups Snow Peas

Method:

In a bowl, combine 2 Tbsp. soy sauce, rice vinegar, and ½ Tbsp. of the arrowroot or cornstarch.

Add steak to the mixture and let marinate for 15 minutes.

In another bowl, combine ½ cup broth with remaining soy sauce, remaining arrowroot or cornstarch, Hoisin sauce, and chili puree; set aside.

Heat half the oil in a wok or skillet. Add the beef and marinade; stir-fry for 3 minutes. Remove the beef and set aside in a bowl.

Heat remaining oil. Add the garlic and ginger, and stir-fry for 30 seconds.

Add the celery, broccoli, and red pepper. Add the remaining broth. Cover. Steam 2 to 3 minutes.

Add the snow peas and cook 1 to 2 minutes more. The vegetables should be crisp.

Add in the sauce and cook 1 minute.

Add in the beef and serve.

Macronutrients (per serve):

Protein: 19g

Carbs: 12g

Fat:7g

Calories 185

Protein Pumpkin Pie

Serves: 1

Preparation time: 5 minutes

Cooking time: 45 minutes

Chilling Time: 5 hours

Ingredients:

½ cup (125ml) canned Pumpkin or Butternut Squash

6oz (175ml) non-fat Greek Yogurt

1 egg

1 Tbsp (15ml) Protein Powder

Cinnamon or Pumpkin Pie Spice to taste.

Method:

Pre-heat oven to 375°F (190°C).

Spray a medium-sized round with non-stick spray.

Mix all the ingredients together and pour into baking dish.

Bake for 45 minutes.

Refrigerate overnight or 4-5 hours.

Macronutrients:

Protein: 31g

Carbs: 19g

Fat: 5g

Calories: 245

Baked Chicken

Serves: 6

Preparation time: 5 minutes

Cooking time: 20 minutes

Ingredients:

6 large boneless skinless Chicken Breasts

1½ cups (375ml) Chicken Broth

¾ tsp (4ml) Onion Powder

¾ tsp (4ml) Garlic Salt

Fresh Ground Black Pepper to taste

Method:

Preheat oven to 350°F (180°C)

Rinse, and pat chicken breasts dry.

Spray a small, shallow baking dish with cooking spray.

Sprinkle chicken with onion powder, garlic salt, and pepper.

Place in baking dish.

Add chicken broth to dish.

Bake 20 minutes or until no longer pink.

Macronutrients (per serve):

Protein: 25.4g

Carbs: 0.7g

Fat: 3.2g

Calories 141.3

Turkey Power Balls

Serves: 6 (2 power balls per serve)

Preparation time: 10 minutes

Cooking time: 25 minutes

Ingredients:

40oz (1.13Kg) Lean Ground Turkey

2 large Eggs Whites

6 Portobello Mushrooms

Dill Weed

Seasoned Italian Herbs

2 slices of Monterey Jack cheese

Black Pepper

A pinch of Sea Salt

Method:

Pre-heat the oven to 320°F (110°C)

Peel and dice the Portobello mushrooms and add into a large mixing bowl

Add the ground turkey into the bowl along with a tablespoon each of Dill Weed and Italian Herbs. Add a ½ teaspoon of black pepper and a pinch of sea salt.

Crack the eggs and separate the whites from the yolk. Add the whites into the bowl.

Mix everything with your hands, ensuring that there is even distribution of all ingredients throughout the mixture.

Once mixed, tear small pieces of the Monterey Jack cheese and add it in evenly to the mix.

Spray a baking tray with non-stick spray

Roll the mixture into 12 golf-sized balls and place on tray.

Place in oven and leave for approximately 18-22 minutes until slightly browned.

Macronutrients (per serve):

Protein: 47g

Carbs: 0g

Fat: 5.4g

Calories 230

Honey Nut Barbeque Chicken Fingers

Serves: 2

Preparation time: 10 minutes

Cooking time: 15 minutes

Ingredients:

6 skinless Chicken Breast tenders

½ cup (125ml) Fiber One Honey Clusters, crushed

½ cup (125ml) ground Honey Roasted Almonds

2 Egg Whites, slightly beaten

1 tsp organic barbecue sauce

Pepper to taste

Finely chopped garlic to taste

Method:

Preheat the oven to 450°F (220°C)

In a shallow dish, combine the egg whites and barbecue sauce.

In another dish mix the crushed cereal, ground almonds, garlic and pepper.

Dip the chicken pieces into the egg dish, and then coat with the crumb mixture.

Bake about 12 minutes or until the chicken is fully cooked.

Macronutrients (per serve):

Protein: 35g

Carbs: 14g

Fat: 12g

Calories: 300

Chicken Egg White Pizza

Serves: 1

Preparation time: 5 minutes

Cooking time: 5 minutes

Ingredients:

4oz (115g) Boneless Skinless Chicken Breasts

4 large Egg Whites

¼ cup (63ml) Tomato Sauce

1 cup, (250ml) chopped Peppers, Sweet, Green

2 Tbsp (30ml) Peppers, Sweet, Red

2 Tbsp (30ml)Mexican Style Four Cheese

2 Tbsp (30ml) Onions

Method:

On Medium heat thoroughly cook egg whites in small round pan.

Season with pepper, garlic or any other "pizza-y" seasoning you like.

flip egg whites over and add 1/4 cup tomato sauce, chopped vegetables, grilled chicken and cheese.

Reduce heat to medium low and cook until the cheese is melted on top.

Serve.

Macronutrients:

Protein: 47.4g

Carbs: 17.2g

Fat: 10.8g

Calories: 342

Curry Rice

Serves: 2

Preparation time: 10 minutes

Cooking time: 20 minutes

Ingredients:|

2 cups (500ml) cooked Rice, preferably pre-cooked and refrigerated

200g diced Chicken Breast

100g mixed Frozen Vegetables (substitute with fresh if you prefer)

2 Whole Eggs

1 tsp (5ml) Curry Powder

2 cloves Garlic

5g Ginger

1 Tbsp (15ml) Soy Sauce

1 Tbsp (15ml) Oyster Sauce

Method:

Marinate diced chicken breast in half of the soy sauce and oyster sauce

Fry chicken breast over high heat until cooked. Set this aside

Beat eggs, and make very thin omelets, (makes 3-4 thin omelets). Set these aside after slicing

Add a dash of oil to a hot wok and cook finely chopped garlic cloves + ginger for a few seconds

add pre-cooked rice to the pan

Immediately add curry powder and remaining soy sauce and oyster sauce.

Mix into rice

Add mixed frozen vegetables, omelet and chicken, cook for a couple of minutes then serve

Macronutrients (per serve):

Protein: 36g

Carbs: 82g

Fat: 8g

Salmon Balls

Serves: 5

Preparation time: 5 minutes

Cooking time: 5 minutes

Ingredients:

150g Salmon

80-120g Cottage Cheese

20-35g Breadcrumbs

Method:

Preheat oven to 350°F (180°C)

Put the salmon and cottage cheese in a bowl and mix well.

Roll the salmon in some breadcrumbs and ensure they are well covered.

Bake for 20minutes.

Makes roughly 5 balls.

Macronutrients (per serve):

Protein: 55.1g

Carbs: 17.9g

Fat: 10.2g

Calories: 356

Peanut Butter Chicken

Serves: 1

Preparation time: 70 minutes

Cooking time: 25 minutes

Ingredients:

8oz (230g) Chicken

1 Tbsp (15ml) Peanut Butter

1½ Tbsp (22.5ml) Soy Sauce

Ginger

Garlic powder

Hot sauce

Cayenne pepper (optional)

Method:

Preheat oven to 450°F (220°C)

Mix everything in together except for peanut butter, and let marinate for at least an hour. Place on foil, spread the peanut butter over the chicken.

Cover and bake for 22-25 minutes.

Open and broil for 1 minute.

Macronutrients

Protein: 54g

Carbs: 6g

Fat: 19g

Calories: 440

Baked Pineapple Chicken

Serves: 8

Preparation time: 5 hours

Cooking time: 45 minutes

Ingredients:

3lb (1.4kg) Chicken Breast

20oz (567g) Unsweetened Pineapple Chunks

2 Tbsp (30ml) Sugar Free Syrup

2 Tbsp (30ml) Reduced Sodium Soy Sauce

¼ tsp (2ml) Black Pepper

½ Sweet Onion (around 150g)

½ tsp (2ml) Ground Ginger

1 tsp (5ml) Pure Lemon Juice

3-4 Slices of a Naval Orange

Method:

Chop your onion. Cut your naval orange slices in half.

Combine all of your ingredients together aside from the chicken into a bowl. Mix them together. Add your chicken and mix into a large ziploc bag.

Remove air from bag and mix everything together once the bag is sealed.

Let marinate in the fridge for at least 2-5 hours (overnight works even better).

Preheat oven to 375°F (190°C)

Remove and place into a baking dish. Bake for 45 minutes.

Serve hot.

Macronutrients (per serve):

Protein: 47.25g

Carbs: 11.37g

Fat: 1.37g

Calories: 247

Slow Cooked Chicken Stew

Serves: 10

Preparation time: 15 minutes

Cooking time: 5 hours

Ingredients:

4lb (1.8Kg) Chicken Breast

1 Red Onion, chopped

1 Can (10.75 Ounces/305g) 98% Fat Free Cream of Mushroom Soup

½ tsp (2.5ml) Lemon & Pepper

1½ tsp (7.5ml) Minced Garlic (or 3 Cloves)

1 tsp (5ml) Italian Seasoning

6oz (170g) Mushrooms

2 Large Sweet Potatoes

2 Russet Potatoes

12oz(340g) Carrots

2 Cups (500ml) Water

1 Packet (24g) Onion Gravy Mix

Method:

Chop up your Red Onion, Sweet Potatoes, Russet Potatoes, Carrots, and Mushrooms.

Cut your Chicken Breasts into 1 inch pieces.

Combine all of your ingredients into the slow cooker.

Cook on high for 4-5 hours.

Serve.

Macronutrients (per serve):

Protein: 45.6g

Carbs: 36g

Fat: 3.3g

Calories: 356

Italian Slow Cooked Chicken

Serves: 12

Preparation time: 15 minutes

Cooking time: 8 hours

Ingredients:

4 ½lb (2Kg) Chicken Breast meat

½ tsp (2.5ml) Black Pepper

1 tsp (5ml) Mrs. Dash Italian Medley (or Italian Seasoning)

½ Red Onion, chopped

2 tsp Minced Garlic (4 Cloves)

1 pct (20g) Dry Italian Salad Dressing Mix

1 can (10.5oz / 298g) 98% Fat Free Cream of Mushroom

½ cup (125ml) Water

8oz (240g) Fat Free Cream Cheese

1½ cups (375ml) Baby Bella Mushrooms (around 100g)

Method:

Chop chicken breasts into halves.

Combine all of the ingredients into slow cooker. Stir ingredients together until mixed.

Cook on low for 6-8 hours stirring after 3-4 hours.

Macronutrients (per serve):

Protein: 50g

Carbs: 6g

Fat: 1.75g

Calories: 308

Sloppy Joes

Serves: 7

Preparation time: 10 minutes

Cooking time: 25 minutes

Ingredients:

1 Green Pepper, chopped

1 Red Pepper, chopped

1 Sweet Onion, chopped

2 Carrots, chopped.

1 Tbsp (15ml) Olive Oil

2lb (900g) Lean Ground Beef

1 tsp (5ml) Minced Garlic (or 2 Cloves)

8oz (227g) No Salt Added Tomato Sauce

10 Tbsp (150ml) Hickey & Brown Sugar BBQ Sauce

5 tsp (25ml) Sriracha

1 Tbsp (15ml) Worcestershire sauce

Method:

Heat a skillet over a medium flame and add olive oil.

Add the Green Pepper, Red Pepper, and Sweet Onion, and fry for approximately 3 minutes.

Once cooked add your lean ground beef and brown.

After your beef has browned reduce the burner to low, and add in the rest of your ingredients.

Mix everything together.

Let it simmer on low heat for around 10-15 minutes. Once your sauce starts to thicken up, it's done

Macronutrients (per serve):

Protein: 26.3g

Carbs: 31.6g

Fat: 6.6g

Calories: 251

Creamy Artichoke Chicken

Serves: 2

Preparation time: 10 minutes

Cooking time: 20 minutes

Ingredients:

2 Skinless Chicken Breast

½ cup (125ml) Zoi Greek Yogurt Nonfat Plain Greek Yogurt

6 tsp (30ml) Dijon Mustard

1 cup (250ml) flowerets Broccoli Flower Clusters

½ cup (125ml) Trader Joe's Artichoke Hearts

Method:

Preheat your oven to 350 F (180 C)

Grind the broccoli in a food processor, mix with artichoke hearts, Greek yogurt, and dijon mustard.

Coat top of chicken breasts with the mix. Place in a shallow oven-proof dish.

Bake for 15-20 minutes.

Macronutrients (per serve):

Protein: 38g

Carbs: 16g

Fat: 2g

Calories 242

Spicy Coconut Chicken Tenders

Serves: 2

Preparation time: 10 minutes

Cooking time: 25 minutes

Ingredients:

2 tsp (10ml) Sriracha Hot Chili Sauce

4 oz (135g) Chicken Breast Tenderloins

4 Tbsp (60ml) raw Unsweetened Shredded Coconut

2 Tbsp (30ml) All Whites 100% Liquid Egg Whites

12 oz (355g) Chicken Breast

Method:

Preheat the oven to 350F(180 C)

Place the shredded coconut on a plate and spread it out some.

Mix the liquid egg whites and sriracha together.

Dip the raw chicken in this mix. Then roll the tenders on a plate that has the coconut shreds on it. Repeat this process and make certain the chicken tenders are well covered.

Spray a baking tray with non-stick spray, ensure that it is well covered.

Place the chicken on the baking sheet and bake for 25 minutes.

Recommended Toppings:

Sriracha

Cinnamon

Macronutrients (per serve):

Protein: 26g

Carbs: 7g

Fat: 13g

Calories: 260

Peanut Butter Chicken

Serves: 1

Preparation time: 5 minutes

Cooking time: 5 minutes

Ingredients:

5oz (150 g) Chicken Breast

½ Onion, medium, chopped

100 ml Almond Milk

20 g Peanut Butter

1 clove Garlic

¼ Hot Chili Pepper

1 tsp (5ml) Ginger

1 packet Sweeteners (Splenda, Sucralose)

Method:

Fry onion and chicken breast on a medium heat until just cooked

While chicken an onion is cooking, mix up all other ingredients in a blender

When chicken is just cooked, add your sauce into the hot pan and bring to a boil, simmering to desired consistency

Macronutrients:

Protein: 50g

Carbs: 14g

Fat: 23g

Calories: 467

Chicken Avocado Burger Patties

Serves: 4

Preparation time: 5 minutes

Cooking time: 5 minutes

Ingredients:

½ cup (125ml) Cilantro

1 Tbsp (15ml) Onion Powder

¼ tsp (1ml) Black Pepper

1 Avocado

1 Tbsp (15ml) Lime Juice

½ cup (125ml) chopped Scallions or Spring Onions

2¼ cups (560ml) Extra Lean Ground Chicken

¼ tsp (1ml) Sea Salt

2 tsp (10ml) Minced Garlic

1 tsp (5ml) Garlic & Herb Seasoning Blend

¼ cup (63ml) Whole Wheat Bread Crumbs

Method:

Preheat oven to 350 F (180 C)

In a large mixing bowl combine all the ingredients together.

Use hands to mix ingredients, turning and mixing thoroughly.

Form 4 med sized patties with hands and put on baking sheet.

Cook on one side for 18-20 min, flip and cook other side for same amount.

Serve and enjoy.

Macronutrients (per serve):

Protein: 27g

Carbs: 13g

Fat: 16g

Calories: 302

Tuna Melt

Serves: 1

Preparation time: 5 minutes

Cooking time: 5 minutes

Ingredients:

½ can (6.5 oz), Tuna chunks in Water, drained

2 slices Arnold Low Carb Multi Grain Bread

1 Tbsp (15ml) Fat Free Mayonnaise

2 slices Borden Fat Free Single Cheese Slices

A pinch Morton Sea Salt

Dash Black Pepper

1 tsp (5ml) Texas Pete Hot Sauce

Method:

Mix all ingredients together in a bowl except the cheese and bread.

Place cheese on bread and mixture followed by other bread slice and toast until cheese has melted.

Serve hot.

Macronutrients:

Protein: 40g

Carbs: 27g

Fat: 5g

Calories: 290

Chicken Pot Pie

Serves: 10

Preparation time: 15 minutes

Cooking time: 6 hours

Ingredients:

5lb (2.25Kg) Chicken Breast

3 Cans (32.25 Ounces/915g) Healthy Request/Fat Free Cream of Chicken Soup

1 Can (10 3/4 Ounces/305g) 98% Fat Free Cream of Celery

1 Can (10 3/4 Ounces/305g) 98% Fat Free Cream of Mushroom

1½ tsp (7.5ml) Black Pepper

1 tsp (5ml) Garlic Salt

1 tsp (5ml) Onion Powder

5 Packets/Cubes Low/No Sodium Chicken Bouillon

1½ cups (375ml) Sliced Mushrooms

1 cup (250ml) Chopped Celery

1 cup (250ml) Chopped Carrots

16oz (470ml) Frozen Mixed Vegetables

8 Medium Red Potatoes

Method:

Chop up Celery, Carrots, and Red Potatoes.

Cut your Chicken Breasts in half. Combine all of your ingredients into the slow cooker.

Mix everything together.

Cook on high for 5-6 hours.

Macronutrients (per serve):

Protein: 69g

Carbs: 43.9g

Fat: 4.7g

Calories: 494

Spicy Chicken Lentils

Servings: 8

Preparation time: 10 minutes

Cooking time: 6 hours

Ingredients:

3½lb (1.57kg) Chicken Breasts

1½ Tbsp (22.5ml) Olive Oil

1½ tsp (7.5ml) Minced Garlic (or 3 Cloves)

1 Sweet Onion

6oz (170g) Carrots

1 tsp (5ml) Basil

1½ cups (375ml) Lentils

4 tbsp (60ml) Sriracha

1 cup (250ml) BBQ Sauce

2 cups (500ml) Water

Method:

Take out your chicken breasts, trim off the fat , and cut into halves.

Chop up your sweet onion and carrots.

Combine everything into your slow cooker.

Cook on low for 6 hours.

Macronutrients (per serve):

Protein: 63g

Carbs: 39.75g

Fat: 4.13g

Calories: 448

Spicy Turkey Chili

Serves: 1

Preparation time: 7 minutes

Cooking time: 10 minutes

Ingredients:

4oz (120g) Extra-lean Ground Turkey

¾ cup (180ml) Black Beans

½ cup (125ml) Corn (steamed)

1 packet McCormick's Chili

⅓ cup (83ml) Tomato Paste

⅓ cup (83ml) diced Tomatoes

¼ cup (63ml) chopped Fresh Basil (optional)

1 Jalapeno Pepper (diced, optional)

Seasonings to taste:

½ Tbsp (7.5ml) each Paprika, Cumin, Cayenne, Pepper

Cheese (optional): 1 oz (30g) Goat, Feta, or Low-fat Mozzarella Cheese

Method:

Season ground turkey with paprika, cumin, cayenne, and pepper.

Set a skillet on medium heat and lightly spray with coconut oil. Add meat.

Chop the meat as it cooks in the skillet using a spatula. When the meat is nearly cooked, add in the chili seasoning and tomato paste. Stir.

Add black beans (with some juice), corn, basil, and any other vegetables.

Reduce the skillet to low heat and cover. Let it simmer and cook for 8-10 minutes.

Remove the skillet from the heat and let it cool. Top with cheese if desired.

Macronutrients:

Protein: 46g

Carbs: 50g

Fat: 3g

Calories 395

Rotisserie Chicken Noodle Pasta Bake

Serves: 1

Preparation time: 10 minutes

Cooking time: 25 minutes

Ingredients:

4oz (120g) cooked rotisserie Chicken (pulled)

⅓ cup (83ml) Whole Wheat or Durum Wheat Pasta Shells

½ up (125ml) Chicken Broth

1 Tbsp (15ml) 2% Greek Yogurt

¼ cup (63ml) diced Carrots

¼ cup (63ml) chopped Celery

¼ cup (63ml) diced Mushrooms (optional)

Fresh parsley

Seasonings to taste:

1 tsp (5ml) each cumin, pepper, garlic, onion powder, Mrs. Dash poultry seasoning

Method:

Preheat oven to 405 F (210 C).

In a pot, boil and cook your wheat pasta. Rinse and set aside.

Dice your raw carrots and mushrooms.

Weigh and separate 4 oz baked chicken meat. In a small disposable ramekin or baking dish, add chicken, pasta, Greek yogurt, veggies, and seasonings. Stir with a spoon or mini-spatula.

Pour chicken broth over the mixture. Ensure that a majority of the noodles are covered so that they won't burn when baking.

Top with fresh parsley.

Bake in the oven for 20-25 minutes. Remove from the oven and enjoy.

Macronutrients:

Protein: 39g

Carbs: 33g

Fat: 3g

Calories 347

Teriyaki Salmon

Servings: 3

Preparation time: 60 minutes

Cooking time: 10 minutes

Ingredients:

2 Tbsp (30ml) Olive Oil

3 Tbsp (45ml) Soy Sauce

3 Tbsp (45ml) Sugar-Free Ketchup

2 Tbsp (30ml) Onion Soup Mix Powder

1 Tbsp (15ml) Splenda

½ tsp (2.5ml) minced Garlic

¼ tsp (1ml) Onion Powder

Three 6-oz. (360g) Salmon Steaks

Method:

Combine olive oil, soy sauce, sugar-free ketchup, onion soup mix powder, and Splenda in a bag.

Place salmon filets in the bag and then let sit for about an hour to marinate.

Remove filets from bag and place on the grill for 4-5 minutes per side.

Serve with freshly-steamed vegetables and quinoa or brown rice.

Macronutrients (per serve):

Protein: 46.6g

Carbs: 5.9g

Fat: 7g

Calories: 363

Field of Greens

Serves: 1

Preparation time: 5 minutes

Cooking time: 5 minutes

Ingredients:

8oz (160g) pasture raised Veal

Sea salt

Chives

Ghee

3 cups Romaine lettuce

1 Tbsp (15ml) Macadamia Nut oil

1 tsp (5ml) Balsamic Vinegar

Method:

Heat ghee in skillet to coat the pan. Insert veal. Season with salt and chives.

Brown meat and flip a few times it cooks pretty quick on medium heat for about 10 minutes.

Toss romaine with oil and vinegar; serve immediately.

Macronutrients:

Protein: 51g

Carbs: 8g

Fat: 2g

Calories: 296

Lobster Boat

Serves: 1

Preparation time: 5 minutes

Cooking time: None

Ingredients:

6-8oz (170g) Lobster (ideally claw meat)

1 Tbsp (15ml) light Mayonnaise

Juice from 1/4 Lemon

¼ Bell Pepper, diced

¼ Onion, diced

1 stalk Celery, diced

3-4 Romaine Lettuce heart leaves

Salt and Pepper and other spices, to taste

Method:

Remove lobster meat from shell and cut or tear into chunks. Place in a bowl.

Add diced vegetables to the lobster then mix in the mayo, lemon juice, and spices.

Fill the Romaine heart leaves with lobster salad.

Serve

Macronutrients:

Protein: 42g

Carbs: 8g

Fat: 6g

Calories: 260

Spicy Turkey Meatballs

Serves: 4

Preparation time: 10 minutes

Cooking time: 20 minutes

Ingredients:

1½lb (675g) ground Turkey

1 large Egg

2 large Egg whites

¾ cup (180ml) Oats

2 Tbsp. (30ml) minced Jalapeno Pepper

½ tsp (2.5ml) Chili Pepper

¼ cup (63ml) Salsa

½ finely diced green Bell Pepper

½ finely diced red Bell Pepper

Directions:

Preheat oven to 450 F (230 C).

Using your hands, combine all ingredients together in a large bowl.

Form mixture into medium-sized meatballs.

Set meatballs in a baking dish.

Place dish in oven and cook for 12-15 minutes, or until golden brown.

Top with added salsa.

Macronutrients:

Protein: 19g

Carbs: 7.2g

Fat: 1.7g

Calories: 121

Chicken Cheese Meatballs

Serves: Multiple

Preparation time: 5 minutes

Cooking time: 10 minutes

Ingredients

1½lb (675g) ground Chicken Breast

½ cup (125ml) Low-Fat Mozzarella Cheese

½ cup (125ml) Low-Fat Parmesan Cheese

1 Tbsp (15ml) Oregano

3 Egg Whites

1 cup (250ml) Oats

½ cup (125ml) finely diced Onion

Directions

Preheat oven to 450 F (230 C).

Using your hands, combine all ingredients.

Roll chicken mixture into bite-sized meatballs.

Place meatballs on a greased baking sheet.

Bake for 8-10 minutes or until golden brown.

Macronutrients (per meatball):

Protein: 19.6g

Carbs: 7.2g

Fat: 4.3g

Calories: 155

Chicken Caesar Meatballs

Serves: 10

Preparation time: 10 minutes

Cooking time: 30 minutes

Ingredients

1½lb (675g) ground chicken

3 egg whites

1 cup (250ml) Oats

2 Tbsp (30ml) Low-Fat Caesar salad dressing

½ minced clove Garlic

4 Tbsp (60ml) Low-Fat Parmesan cheese

Directions

Preheat oven 425 F (220 C).

Combine all ingredients in a large bowl.

Roll chicken mixture into about 20 meatballs.

Place each meatball in a muffin cup and bake for 25-28 minutes, or until golden brown.

Once out of the oven, remove from muffin tin.

Before serving, squeeze lemon juice over top.

Macronutrients:

Protein: 19g

Carbs: 7.2g

Fat: 2.8g

Calories: 129

Fish in Foil

Serves: 1

Preparation time: 5 minutes

Cooking time: 20 minutes

Ingredients:

4 oz (120g) Tilapia

Asparagus

½ Lemon, sliced

Juice of ½ a Lemon

Fish seasoning

Pepper

Method:

Preheat oven to375 F (190 C)

Use one piece of foil per fish.

Add lemon juice.

Sprinkle fish seasoning on top.

Add pepper, lemon slices.

Add veggies on top.

Fold into foil down from the top leaving air for steaming

Place each foil on a cookie sheet and bake for 15-20 minutes.

Macronutrients:

Protein: 30g

Carbs: 11g

Fat: 5g

Calories: 209

Chicken Cucumber Salad

Serves: 1

Preparation time: 10 minutes

Cooking time: none

Ingredients:

1 Cucumber

2 stalks of Celery

30g Red Onion

70g Spinach and Kale Greek Yogurt dip

30g Fat-Free Cheddar Cheese

1 can of Chunk Chicken, drained (about 185g)

Directions:

Peel and chop the cucumber, celery, and onion.

Combine all ingredients in a large mixing bowl.

Season to taste

Serve

Macronutrients:

Protein: 51g

Carbs: 19g

Fat: 10g

Calories: 377

Sweet Potato Omelet

Serves: 1

Preparation time: 7 minutes

Cooking time: 10 minutes

Ingredients:

3 large Whole Eggs

1 medium Sweet Potato, baked

3 slices lean Turkey Bacon

¼ (63ml) cup Shredded Cheese

1 Tbsp (15ml) Low-Fat Sour Cream

Method:

Peel sweet potato and mash the flesh. Reheat it in a skillet or in the microwave.

Cook turkey bacon in a skillet to taste.

Once turkey is done, scramble the eggs and pour them into a non-stick skillet set to medium heat. Cover the entire skillet surface in a thin layer of egg. Let the eggs set and then carefully flip it over.

Spread sweet potato on one side of the eggs.

Sprinkle cheese on top of sweet potato.

Place bacon on top of cheese and sweet potato.

Spread sour cream on top of bacon.

Fold eggs in half and let sit for a minute or two.

Flip omelet over and let sit for a minute or two.

Remove from heat and place on plate.

Add salt and pepper as desired and enjoy!

Macronutrients:

Protein: 37g

Carbs: 27gg

Fat: 24g

Calories: 485

Thai Spicy Beef Salad

Serves: 1

Preparation time: 10 minutes

Cooking time: 5-10 minutes

Ingredients:

½lb (225g) lean Steak

Salt and pepper, to taste

4 cups (1ℓ) Mixed Greens

2 Tbsp (30ml) each: fresh Mint, Basil, and Cilantro

2 green Onions, sliced

2 Tbsp (30ml) fresh Lime Juice

½ tsp (2.5ml) Lemongrass paste or fresh Lemongrass

1 tsp (5ml) low sodium Soy Sauce

1 tsp (5ml) Chili Flakes

2 tsp (10ml) Fish Sauce

1/2 tsp (2.5ml) Stevia in the Raw

Method:

Season steak with salt and pepper and grill to desired readiness.

In a small bowl, mix greens, mint, basil, and cilantro.

In another small bowl, mix lemongrass, green onions, lime juice, soy sauce, fish sauce, chili flakes, and Stevia.

Slice steak and place on top of greens.

Pour dressing over greens and steak.

Toss lightly and serve.

Macronutrients:

Protein: 36g

Carbs: 18g

Fat: 7g

Calories: 260

Malaysian Curry Prawns

Serves: 4

Preparation time: 10 minutes

Cooking time: 10 minutes

Ingredients:

½lb (225g) large Prawns, with shell/tail

1 Tbsp (15ml) Coconut Oil

1 Tbsp (15ml) fresh Garlic, chopped

1 can light Coconut Milk

1 Tbsp (15ml) Curry Powder

Salt and pepper, to taste

Method:

De-vein the prawns.

Heat coconut oil in large pan over medium high heat and add the garlic.

Rinse prawns and lightly salt and pepper.

Add prawns to pan and sprinkle with curry powder.

Sauté for 2-3 minutes until all prawns are well-seasoned.

Add coconut milk and turn heat to low.

Simmer for 5 minutes.

Serve.

Macronutrients (per serve):

Protein: 15g

Carbs: 4g

Fat: 11g

Calories 172

Chicken Curry

Serves: 2

Preparation time: 7 minutes

Cooking time: 10 minutes

Ingredients:

5oz (150g) boneless Chicken Breast

5 cups (1.25ℓ) sliced raw Mushroom

1 whole Red Pepper

2 cups (250ml) green raw Snap Beans

¼ cup (83ml) canned Chicken Broth

1 cups (250ml) Low-Fat Yogurt

4 tsp (20ml) Cornstarch

4 tsp (20ml) Extra Virgin Olive Oil

2 tsp (10ml) Curry Powder

Method:

Take chicken breasts and cut into medium sized cubes. Grab a large non-stick deep frying pan and add the chicken breasts with 1 tablespoon of olive oil. Cook the chicken in frying pan until its browned and done.

While the chicken is cooking grab another non-stick frying pan and add mushrooms, pepper, and beans with 2 tablespoons of olive oil. Stir this mixture regularly until its soft.

Back to the first pan and add chicken broth, yogurt, curry powder, and cornstarch. Stir this mixture regularly until the sauce thickens. Increase heat if needed.

Macronutrients:

Protein: 32g

Carbs: 735g

Fat: 13g

Calories: 373

Beef Chop Suey

Serves: 1

Preparation time: 5 minutes

Cooking time: 15 minutes

Ingredients:

7oz (210g) Beef, fat trimmed.

6 large Egg Whites

1 large Onion, chopped

3 cups (750ml) Danish raw cabbage

2½ stripes Celery

2 cups (500ml) of thin sliced Mushrooms

1½ cups (375ml) mature Soybean

2 cups (500ml) Chinese canned Water Chestnut

2 tsp (10ml) Olive Oil

2 Tbsp (60ml) Apple Cider Vinegar

1 Tbsp (15ml) Soy Sauce

½ cup (125ml) broth bouillon canned, ready to serve beef

Method:

You will need 2 large non-stick frying pans. In the first frying pan add the olive oil and beef and cook until the beef is brown. Don't cook for too long, the beef will go tough and chewy.

While the beef is cooking, in the second frying pan, add 2 tablespoons of olive oil, cabbage, celery, mushrooms, water chestnuts, soybean, vinegar and onion. Cook until entire mixture is hot, and the onions have softened.

Now add the soy sauce, beef stock and cooked beef. Cook this mixture for 5-10 minutes.

Macronutrients:

Protein: 50g

Carbs: 38g

Fat: 16g

Calories: 490

Salsa Quinoa Chicken

Serves: 5

Preparation time: 5 minutes

Cooking time: 5 minutes

Ingredients:

2 cups (500ml) Quinoa, uncooked

24oz (720g) cooked Chicken

2 cups (500ml) Salsa

1 cup (250ml) Onion, chopped

Diced Jalapeno to taste (optional)

Method:

Boil quinoa in with 4 cups water. After reaching a raging boil, turn the heat down to medium-low. Allow quinoa to cook until only a slight amount of water is left. Pull quinoa from heat, and let stand covered for 10 minutes. Extra water will soak into the quinoa.

Mix chicken, salsa and onion in with the quinoa.

Divide evenly into 5 Tupperware containers.

Macronutrients:

Protein: 40g

Carbs: 49g

Fat: 6g

Calories: 434

Grilled Tuna Burgers

Serves: 4

Preparation time: 10 minutes

Cooking time: 10 minutes

Ingredients:

450g Tuna

40g Onion, chopped

1 large Carrot, shredded

2 cloves Garlic, finely chopped

4 Egg Whites

20g chopped Chives

40g Bread Crumbs

Spices to taste

Method:

Mix all the ingredients together in a large mixing bowl.

Split ingredients into four patties.

Take a tray and cover with a non-stick piece of baking paper.

Spray the paper lightly with low fat cooking spray.

Grill patties on both sides until brown.

Serve either with a roll and trimmings, or with rice and vegetables.

Macronutrients:

Protein: 35g

Carbs: 15g

Fat: 1.2g

Calories: 200

Tuna Cheese Melt

Serves: 1

Preparation time: 9 minutes

Cooking time: 6 minutes

Ingredients:

1 5oz (150g) can of Tuna,

2 Tbsp (30ml) of Oatmeal

1 Egg White

Diced Onion to taste

Fresh, minced Garlic to taste

⅓oz (10g) Mozzarella or Cheddar cheese

Salt and Pepper to taste

Method:

Place all ingredients into a mixing bowl.

Mix, or mash ingredients together, and form into a patty.

Place patty into a frying pan, and cook over medium heat.

Cook until slightly brown on both sides.

Macronutrients:

Protein: 26g

Carbs: 4g

Fat: 2g

Calories: 145

Thai Spiced Chicken

Serves: 4

Preparation time: Overnight

Cooking time: 40 minutes

Ingredients:

6 Chicken Breasts cut in half

12oz (350g) natural Non-Fat or Low-Fat Yogurt

2-3 Tbsp (15ml) Thai Red Curry Paste

4 Tbsp (60ml) chopped fresh Cilantro

3 inch (7.5 cm) piece Cucumber

Lime Wedges and Salad Greens to serve

Method:

Preheat your oven to 375 F (190 C).

Put the chicken in a shallow dish in one layer. Blend a third of the yogurt, the curry paste and three tablespoons of the cilantro. Season well with salt and pour over the chicken, turning the pieces until they are evenly coated. Leave for at least 10 minutes, or in the fridge overnight.

Lift the chicken on to a rack in a roasting tin and roast for 35-40 minutes, until golden.

Blend together the remaining yogurt and cilantro. Finely chop the cucumber and stir into the yogurt mixture. Season. Serve with the chicken and garnish with wedges of lime and salad greens.

Macronutrients (per serve):

Protein: 43g

Carbs: 8g

Fat: 3g

Calories: 166

Snacks & Desserts

Peanut Butter Chocolate Protein Cookies

Chocolate Protein Frozen Yogurt Recipe

Strawberry, Banana and Peanut Butter Ice Cream

Chocolate Orange Protein Balls

Peanut Butter Oatmeal Raisin Muffins

High Protein Chocolate Cake

Rice Pudding

Protein Brownies

Protein Snickers

Peanut Butter Chocolate Cookies

Peanut Butter Ice Cream

Chocolate Mug Cake

Protein Bars

Strawberry and Banana Protein Bar

Banana Bread

Cookies and Cream Rice Krispy Treat

Honey Nut Protein Bars

Peanut Butter Cup Cakes

Protein Oreos

Protein Brownies

High Protein Cheesecake

Chocolate Peanut Butter Protein Bars

Chocolate Peanut Butter Cookie Dough

Protein Pudding

Protein Truffles

Chocolate Cake

Cottage Cheesecake

Amino Acid Jelly

Delicious Dessert Pizza

Chocolate Peanut Butter Wrap

Strawberry Fluff

Banana Flaxseed Muffins

Protein Pancakes/Strawberry Shortcake

Protein Lava Brownie

Protein Mousse Recipe

Protein Cookies and Cream Waffles

Gluten Free Protein Carrot Cake

Boston Cream Donut

Apple Pie Protein Donut

Blueberry Protein Donuts

Chocolate Protein Donuts

Protein Packed Parfait

Coconut-Oat Bars

Cinnamon Scroll

Strawberry Cheesecake

Peanut Butter Chocolate Protein Cookies

Servings: 18

Preparation time: 10 minutes

Cooking time: 2 minutes

Chilling time 1 Hour

Ingredients:

3 cups (750ml) Puffed Brown Rice

1 scoop (30g) Whey Protein Powder (any flavor)

1 cup (250ml) Oats

¼ cup (63ml) Nuts/Dried Fruit

¼ cup (63ml) Stevia

6 tsp (20ml) Dark unsweetened Cocoa

½ cup (125ml) Honey

1 tsp (5ml) Vanilla Extract

¾ cup (180ml) organic Peanut Butter

Method:

Pour 3 cups of brown puffed rice into a mixing bowl.

Add 1 scoop of whey protein

Add 1 cup of whole oats and add some crushed nuts or dried fruit of your choice

In a microwavable bowl.

Combine Stevia, peanut butter, honey and vanilla extract.

Place in the microwave for 30 second intervals, stirring frequently, until combined.

Add peanut butter mixture of the crispy rice and stir until well mixed!

Shape mixture into cookies and place in fridge for an hour

Macronutrients (per serve):

Protein: 5.6g

Carbs: 21.5g

Fat: 7g

Calories: 153

Chocolate Protein Frozen Yogurt

Serves: 1

Preparation time: 5 minutes

Chilling time: 60 minutes

Ingredients:

1 Banana (fresh or frozen)

100g of Full-Fat organic natural live Yogurt

1 Tbsp (15ml) Green & Black's organic Cocoa

40g of Chocolate Protein Powder

Method:

Place the banana, cocoa and protein powder in the blender and blend until even and crumbly

Add in the yogurt and blend

Pour in to a bowl, jar or dish and freeze for 30-60 minutes.

Test it with your finger on the top to check how far gone it is.

Macronutrients:

Protein: 41g

Carbs: 31g

Fat: 6g

Calories: 350

Strawberry, Banana and Peanut Butter Ice Cream

Serves: 1

Preparation time: 5 minutes

Cooking time: None

Ingredients:

1 frozen Banana

4 frozen Strawberries

1 Tbsp (15ml) of organic Peanut Butter

Method:

Blend frozen banana on a low speed setting in your blender.

Once banana is well blended, add the 4 frozen strawberries and tablespoon of peanut butter.

Macronutrients:

Protein: 10g

Carbs: 15g

Fat: 10g

Calories: 100

Chocolate Orange Protein Balls

Serves: 1

Preparation time: 5 minutes

Cooking time: 5 minutes

Ingredients:

80g Dates

70g Rolled Oats

50g Peanut Butter

3 scoops (90g) of Chocolate Whey Protein

10g Cocoa

1 Orange

1 sachet powdered Egg Whites

20g shredded Coconut

Method:

Finely grate the rind from your orange and add the rind along with everything but the coconut in to your blender. Add in the juice one half of the orange (65ml).

Whizz intermittently until everything comes together in a soft, balling, sticky fashion.

Put your shredded coconut in to a small bowl. The mix is very sticky, I used a tablespoon to remove around 35g of mixture at a time. Plop one spoonful in to the bowl of coconut and tumble it until covered. You can then remove it and roll it in to a ball with your hands.

Plop, roll and ball 10 times. Try and make them even. I sat my bowl on a scale so I could check how much each blob I removed weighed.

Sit the rolled balls on a plate and fridge them for an hour minimum.

Can then store or eat up as desired!

Macronutrients:

Protein: 10g

Carbs: 14g

Fat: 4g

Calories: 131

Macronutrients (per serve):

Protein: 5g

Carbs: 6g

Fat:0.5g

Calories: 48

High Protein Chocolate Cake

Servings: 8

Preparation time: 10 minutes

Cooking time:30 minutes

Ingredients:

2 scoops (60g) Chocolate Whey Protein

½ cup (125ml) Whole Wheat Flour

⅓ cup (83ml) unsweetened Cocoa Powder

1 tsp (5ml) Baking Powder

1 tsp (5ml) Baking Soda

1 egg

2 tsp (5ml) Vanilla extract

¼ cup (63ml) Avocado

1 6oz jar baby food fruit + oatmeal mix

Sweetener of choice (splenda/stevia etc.)

Method:

Preheat oven to 350 F (180 C).

Coat baking pan with cooking spray

Mix all dry ingredients in a separate bowl

Slowly add wet mixture into dry ingredient bowl

Blend bowl of ingredients

Bake for 25 minutes

Macronutrients (per serve):

Protein: 8g

Carbs: 14g

Fat:1.8g

Calories: 120

Rice Pudding

Serves: 1

Preparation time: 5 minutes

Cooking time: 5 minutes

Ingredients:

1½ (375ml) cups cooked White Rice

8 oz (230ml) Vanilla Rice Milk

2 Tbsp (30ml) Lactose Free Chocolate or Vanilla Breyer's Ice Cream

Method:

Place rice in a bullet, or farberware blender, not a regular blender, add rice milk, and ice cream

Blend till thick, open blender, stir, and add more rice milk till full

Blend again till creamy/

Macronutrients:

Protein: 35g

Carbs: 78g

Fat:4g

Calories: 490

Protein Brownies

Serves: 9

Preparation time: 15 minutes

Chilling time: 4 minutes

Ingredients:

2 scoops (60g) Vanilla Whey

30g chopped Almonds

3g Cocoa Powder

50g Oats

50ml Almond Milk

30g Roasted Peanuts

3 Tbsp (45ml) crunchy Peanut Butter

Dark chocolate coated thin Rice Cakes for base

90g 60% Dark Chocolate

Method:

Place some rice cakes on an aluminum foil these form the base for the chocolate bites.

Mix all the powders and oats together in a bowl.

Add in the peanut butter and almond milk and stir until you get a thick batter.

Add in the almonds and stir a bit more to mix.

Coat the rice thins with the mixture and spread evenly across the whole base.

Place tray in freezer for 15 minutes until you melt the dark chocolate in a Bain Marie.

Once the dark choc is melted, take the tray out of the freezer. Before pouring the chocolate, place the roasted peanuts on top of the hardened mixture.

Pour the dark chocolate on top and spread evenly with a spatula or spoon.

Place in the fridge for 3-4 hours to get everything firm.

Remove and cut into equal squares.

Macronutrients (per serve):

Protein: 11g

Carbs: 13g

Fat:11g

Calories: 190

Protein Snickers

Serves: 10

Preparation time: 10 minutes

Cooking time: 2 minutes

Ingredients:

Filling

100g Peanut Butter

50g Protein Powder

10g Cocoa

200g Low Fat Greek Yogurt

20g crushed raw Peanuts

Chocolate shell:

80g +85% Chocolate

20g Coconut Oil

Sweetener

Method:

Protein bar:

Mix all ingredients together.

Divide the mixture into 10 equal parts, and shape into a bars

Chocolate cover:

Break the chocolate into small pieces

Melt the coconut oil, (Place container in boiling water,)

Melt the chocolate, add the coconut oil and whisk

Coat the bars with a small amount of chocolate, dip them in the chocolate

Macronutrients (per serve):

Protein: 10.2g

Carbs: 3.5g

Fat: 11.3g

Calories: 156

Peanut Butter Chocolate Cookies

Servings: 8

Preparation time: 5 minutes

Cooking time: 10 minutes

Ingredients:

60g Protein Powder

75ml Almond Milk

3 Tbsp (45ml) of smooth Peanut Butter

15g chopped Almonds

30g Oats

60g Dark Chocolate (60%)

Method:

Preheat oven to 212 F (100 C).

Mix the first 2 ingredients thoroughly. Then add the peanut butter and continue to blend until smooth.

Mix this paste with the oats and almonds and with a spoon and stir well.

Fold in the chopped dark chocolate (or chocolate chips).

Form balls out of the mixture and place on cooking tray.

Bake for 5 minutes and then switch off oven and leave for another 2-3 minutes.

Remove and leave them on the tray to cool.

Macronutrients (per serve):

Protein: 8g

Carbs: 8g

Fat: 7g

Calories 127

Peanut Butter Ice Cream

Serves: 1

Preparation time: 5 minutes

Cooking time: 30 minutes

Ingredients:

100ml Low Fat Milk

3 Tbsp (45ml) of Crispy Peanut Butter

1 scoop (30g) Vanilla Whey Protein

Method:

Mix milk, Peanut Butter and Whey Protein. Heat it in a pan for 3-4min (until it's creamy).

Place it into the freezer for about 30min.

Macronutrients:

Protein: 38.6g

Carbs: 10.8g

Fat: 22.6g

Calories: 400

Chocolate Mug Cake

Serves: 1

Preparation time: 3 minutes

Cooking time: 1 minutes

Ingredients:

1 Egg White

1 scoop (30g) Chocolate Protein Whey

1 Tbsp (15ml) Cocoa Powder

1 tsp (5ml) Baking Powder

¼ cup (63ml) water or Coconut milk

Non-stick spray

Method:

Mix ingredients in bowl

Spray mug with non stick spray

Pour ingredients into mug and microwave for 40 seconds

Flip over mug and the cake slides out

Macronutrients:

Protein: 30g

Carbs: 6g

Fat: 3g

Calories: 150

Protein Bars

Serves: Multiple

Preparation time: 5 minutes

Cooking time: 15 minutes

Ingredients:

80gr of Oats

2 scoops (60g) of Vanilla or Strawberry Whey Protein

30gr Peanut Butter

20gr Honey

20gr crushed Walnuts

5-10gr Gojie Berries

Enough water to mix all together into a paste.

Method:

Preheat your oven to 300 F (150 C).

Mix everything into a bowl then put into a trey with cooking paper.

Bake for 12 minutes.

Remove and allow to cool slightly, then cut into bars or cubes.

Macronutrients:

Protein 66g

Carbs 90g

Fats 38g

Calories: 920

Strawberry and Banana Protein Bar

Servings: 6

Preparation time: 10 minutes

Cooking time: 35 minutes

Ingredients:

1 cup (280ml) raw Oatmeal

5 scoops (150g) Strawberry Protein Powder

¼ cup (63ml) Fat-Free Cream Cheese

½ cup (125ml) Non-Fat dry Milk Powder

2 Egg Whites

¼ cup (63ml) Water

1½ Bananas, mashed

2 tsp (10ml) Canola oil

Method:

Preheat oven to 330 F (160 C)

Spray a 9x9 square pan with cooking spray & set aside.

In a medium bowl combine oatmeal, Protein powder & dry milk. Set aside.

In another bowl beat together with an electric hand mixer, cream cheese, egg whites, bananas, water & oil.

Add the oat mixture & continue to beat until the two are combined. Pour batter into the prepared pan.

Bake for 30-35 minutes or until toothpick comes out clean.

Macronutrients (per bar):

Protein 22g

Carbs 22g

Fat 3g

Calories: 203

Banana Bread

Serves: 8

Preparation time: 10 minutes

Cooking time: 50 minutes

Ingredients:

200g almond meal or oatmeal, depending on your carb requirements

1 cup (250ml) Vanilla Protein Powder

1 tsp (5ml) Baking Powder

1 cup (250ml) Greek Yogurt

4 eggs

½ tsp (2,5ml) salt

2 bananas, mashed

Method:

Preheat your oven to 280 F (140 C).

Mix the eggs and yogurt together

Add in the two mashed bananas.

Once this is nice and smooth, add in the dry ingredients and mix well.

Pour the mixture into a loaf tin.

Bake for about 50 minutes.

To check to see if it is done, poke a skewer into the middle of the loaf. When it is done, the skewer should come out clean.

Sever cooled

Macronutrients (per serve):

Protein: 24g

Carbs: 12g

Fat: 18g

Calories: 306

Cookies and Cream Rice Krispy Treat

Serves: 1

Preparation time: 10 minutes

Chilling time: 30 minutes

Ingredients:

39g Rice Krispy Cereal

1 scoop (30g) Cookies and Cream Whey Protein

20g Marshmallow Fluff

5g Honey

50g Greek Yogurt

Method:

Combine Dry (Cereal + Whey) in a bowl

Combine Wet (Yogurt, Honey and Fluff) In a small bowl

Take a small square container and coat with cooking spray and then mix the wet and dry in the larger bowl. When combined together you will then drop the mixture into the square container and level off like a square (Krispy Treat)

Allow to sit in fridge for 20-30 minutes and then enjoy so it will settle and bind together.

Macronutrients:

Protein: 30g

Carbs: 60g

Fat: 2g

Calories: 380

Honey Nut Protein Bars

Servings: 6

Preparation time: 10 minutes

Chilling time: 1 hour

Ingredients:

120g Oats

2 scoops (60g) High Protein Whey

100g Peanuts

4 Tbsp (10ml) Olive Oil

2 Tbsp (10ml) Honey

Method:

Start by blitzing the peanuts up, add olive oil and continue to blitz until you have peanut butter (1-2 minutes depending on crunchy or smooth).

Mix with all other ingredients in bowl until it starts to combine, add more oil if too dry.

Put mixture in 8x8 baking tray, spread/ pat down until fully spread evenly.

Put it in the fridge to firm up for an hour, take it out and divide into bars. I cut mine into six, store in foil in fridge and enjoy.

Macronutrients:

Protein: 14g

Carbs: 20g

Fat: 3.5g

Calories: 301

Peanut Butter Cup Cakes

Serves: 3

Preparation time: 15 minutes

Freezer time: 2 hours

Ingredients:

118g of powdered Peanut Butter (PB2)

110ml semi-Skimmed Milk

24g Bourneville cocoa

10g Candarel granulated sweetener

Method:

Add water to the PB2 powder to make a paste in a separate bowl.

Mix the milk, bournville cocoa, and candarel sweetener together.

Start spooning the PB2 into the mixture until it thickens up and resembles thick melted chocolate: use only half of the PB2 mixture, as the other is used for the filling.

Spray 3 cupcake holders with a nonstick spray.

Line the cupcake holders with the chocolate mixture.

Once the cake holders have been lined with the chocolate mixture, spoon blobs of the leftover PB2 paste into the cake holders.

Add the rest of the chocolate mixture over the PB2 paste.

Leave it in the freezer for around 2 hours and it hardens up like regular chocolate.

Macronutrients (per serve):

Protein: 19.6g

Carbs: 22.1g

Fat: 8g

Calories: 206

Protein Oreos

Servings: 7

Preparation time: 10 minutes

Cooking time: 10 minutes

Ingredients:

1 tbsp (15ml) Vanilla Extract

⅓ cup (83ml) Honey

½ scoop (15g) Dymatize Nutrition Elite Casein - Vanilla

¼ cup (63ml) Greek Yogurt

¼ cup (63ml) Almond Meal

1 cup (250ml) Cocoa Powder (Unsweetened)

1 scoop (30g) Chocolate Whey Protein

1 tsp (5ml) Baking Powder

2 tbsp (30ml) Unsweetened Almond Milk

¼ cup (63ml) Unsweetened Applesauce

1 medium Egg

¼ cup (63ml) Lowfat Cottage Cheese

Method:

Preheat oven to 350 F (180 C).

Combine almond meal, cocoa powder, egg, applesauce, vanilla, honey, baking powder and chocolate protein powder.

Form 14 Oreo sized cookies on a greased pan.

Bake for 10 minutes.

For the frosting

Blend cottage cheese, Greek yogurt, 1/2 tbsp of honey, vanilla casein protein and almond milk, when cookies are cooled, place frosting between the cookies.

Macronutrients (per serve):

Protein: 10g

Carbs: 9g

Fat: 5g

Calories: 121

Protein Brownies

Serves: 1

Preparation time: 3 minutes

Cooking time: 1 minutes

Ingredients:

1 scoop (30g) Chocolate Whey Protein

2 tsp (10ml) of Cocoa Powder

1/4 teaspoon Baking Powder

Method:

Mix together with a little water into a paste and microwave for 1 minute.

Best served with low vanilla fat ice-cream.

Macronutrients:

With 50ml ice-cream:

Protein: 30.4g

Carbs: 38.9g

Fat: 6.7g

Calories: 275

High Protein Cheesecake

Serves: Multiple

Preparation time: 10 minutes

Cooking time: 45 minutes

Ingredients:

3 scoops (90g) High Protein Whey

8oz (230ml) fat free Cream Cheese

6oz (170ml) plain Greek Yogurt

8oz (230ml) Skim Milk

½ cup (125ml) Cottage Cheese

1 egg

½ cup (125ml) Spenda (7 packets)

1 tsp (5ml) Vanilla Extract

2 tsp (10ml) Cinnamon

Method:

Preheat your oven to 350 F (180 C).

Mix everything together

Add some blueberries or strawberries for variation (if desired)

Bake for 45 minutes

Allow to cool and place in the fridge for a few hours until cold..

Serve cold

Macronutrients:

Protein: 151g

Carbs 55g

Fat 10g

Calories: 968

Chocolate Peanut Butter Protein Bars

Serves: 6

Preparation time: 10 minutes

Cooking time: 5 minutes

Ingredients:

1½ cups (375ml) Chocolate Whey Protein powder

¾ cup (180ml) Almond Meal

2 Tbsp (30ml) Cocoa powder

¼ cup (63ml) creamy Peanut Butter

½ cup (125ml) milk

100 g Dark Chocolate

Method:

Mix the first 5 ingredients in a bowl until you get a thick paste-like batter. Divide the batter into 6 portions and shape into bars. Chill in the freezer for a few minutes to harden up a bit.

Melt the chocolate slowly over a double boiler. Once melted, add bars one at a time to coat. Stick back in the freezer and enjoy once the chocolate has hardened.

You can also sub in oat or coconut flour for the almond meal, and any other favorite protein powder flavor you like or have on hand

Macronutrients:

Protein: 19g

Carbs 20g

Fat 22g

Calories: 343

Chocolate Peanut Butter Cookie Dough

Serves: 1

Preparation time: 35 minutes

Cooking time: none

Ingredients:

2 tsp (10ml) Peanut Butter

2 scoops (60g) Chocolate Whey Protein

40-50ml Skim Milk

Method:

Mix peanut butter and whey in a bowl and add milk, a little bit at a time, until you have a cookie dough like consistency, put it in the fridge for half an hour and enjoy chocolate peanut butter cookie dough

Macronutrients:

Protein: 56g

Carbs 6g

Fat 19g

Calories: 419

Protein Pudding

Serves: 1

Preparation time: 5 minutes

Cooking time: 5 minutes

Ingredients:

1 cup (250ml) plain Greek Yogurt

1 scoop (30g) Chocolate Whey

3 Tbsp (45ml) unsweetened Cocoa Powder or to taste

Sweetener of choice (optional)

Method:

Stir in the whey and the cocoa powder until completely blended; you should end up with a thick, dark brown paste, add more cocoa if desired.

Serve.

For an added crunch or sweetness, add some nuts, fruit, raw cocoa nibs, etc.

Alternatively, Put it in the freezer for 1-2 hours for a tasty frozen treat.

Macronutrients:

Protein: 52g

Carbs 17g

Fat: 4g

Calories: 330

Protein Truffles

Serves: 10 (3 balls per serve)

Preparation time: 15 minutes

Cooking time: None

Ingredients:

1 cup (250ml) Defatted Peanut Flour

1 cup (250ml) Vanilla Protein Powder

½ cup (12ml) Splenda

⅓ cup (83ml) Torani SF Vanilla Syrup

2 Tbsp (30ml) Butter

2 Tbsp (30ml) Peanut Butter

1 Tbsp (15ml) Vanilla Extract

Cocoa Powder or Chocolate Chips

Method:

Mix all ingredients until a ball is formed. Add more Splenda if too sticky, more syrup if too dry. Roll into 40 balls.

For Buckeyes, melt chocolate chips and drizzle chocolate over refrigerated, formed, dough balls.

For Truffles, roll formed dough balls in cocoa powder.

Keep refrigerated.

Macronutrients (per serving):

Protein: 80g

Carbs: 12g

Fat: 3g

Calories: 395

Chocolate Cake

Serves: Multiple

Preparation time: 10 minutes

Cooking time: 35 minutes

Ingredients:

1¾ (430ml) cups All-Purpose Flour

½ cup (125ml) Splenda No Calorie Sweetener, Granulated

½ cup (125ml) Splenda Brown Sugar Blend

¾ cup (180ml) cocoa powder

1½ tsp (7,5ml) baking powder

1½ tsp (7,5ml) baking soda

½ (2,5ml) teaspoon salt

1¼ cups (315ml) low-fat buttermilk

¼ cup (63ml) vegetable oil

2 large eggs, lightly beaten

2 tsp (10ml) vanilla extract

1 cup (250ml) hot strong black coffee

Method:

Preheat oven to 350 F (180 C). Grease a 10 cup bund pan with non-stick cooking spray, set aside.

Blend flour, Splenda Granulated Sweetener, Spenda Brown Sugar Blend, baking powder, baking soda, cocoa powder, protein powder and salt in large mixing bowl.

Combine buttermilk, oil, eggs, vanilla extract, and coffee in a small bowl.

Add flour to mixture, using an electric mixer on medium speed, mix until Smooth (about 2 minutes).

Pour batter into cake pan or bundt pan.

Bake for 30-35 minutes, until an inserted toothpick in center of cake comes out clean. Let cool in pan for 5 minutes.

Macronutrients:

Protein: 36g

Carbs 33g

Fat 70g

Calories: 230

Cottage Cheesecake

Serves: 2

Preparation time: 10 minutes

Cooking time: 24 hours

Ingredients:

600g Cottage Cheese

3 large Egg Whites

1 whole large Egg

10 drops (1ml) Vanilla Flavoring

Cinnamon

Method:

Preheat oven to 320F (160C)

Blend all the ingredients in a food processor

Bake for 20-25 minutes. It should still jiggle slightly if you poke the side. Let it cool in the fridge for 6-24 hours then enjoy.

Macronutrients (per serve):

Protein: 42.5g

Carbs: 13g

Fat: 23g

Calories: 423

Amino Acid Jelly

Serves: 1

Preparation time: 5 minutes

Cooking time: 5 minutes

Ingredients:

2 scoops of Scivation Xtend

1½ Tbsp (22.5ml) gelatin

500ml water (plus 100ml for mixing gelatin)

Instructions:

Mix 2 scoops of Xtend into 500ml of cold water and shake.

Separately mix gelatin into 100ml of hot water. Combine gelatin with Xtend mix and shake well.

Pour into a bowl and place in the fridge. Serve when set!

Makes approx 500grms

Macronutrients:

Protein: 15g (Amino Acids)

Carbs: 0

Fat:0

Calories: 60

Delicious Dessert Pizza

Serves: 4

Preparation time: 10 minutes

Cooking time: 5 minutes

Ingredients:

2¼ Cups (563ml) King Arthur Flour" Whole Wheat Organic

2 cups (500ml) Mixed Berries

¼ cup (63ml) Peaches

½ Banana

¼ tsp (1ml) Sea Salt

1 tsp (5ml) Stevia

1 cup (250ml) warm water

Cinnamon

3 Tbsp (45ml) Chocolate Lean beef Aminos

Vanilla Extract

Pizza Crust Yeast

Method:

Preheat your oven to 425 F (200 C).

Dissolve salt, yeast, and stevia in 1 cup of warm water. Then mix flour, cinnamon, vanilla extract with the dissolved salt/yeast/stevia/water mixture. Add the water in increments until a dough like texture is obtained,

Grease a pizza pan.

Wet hands (so dough doesn't stick) spread dough out on pizza pan.

Scatter the Mixed Berries, Peaches, Banana, and Lean beef Aminos over the dough.

Bake for 12 to 15 minutes.

Serve hot

Macronutrients (per serve):

Protein: 15g

Carbs: 42g

Fats: 1.8g

Calories: 334

Chocolate Peanut Butter Wrap

Serves: 1

Preparation time: 5 minutes

Cooking time: None

Ingredients:

1 scoop (30g) Chocolate Protein Powder

1 Tbsp. (15ml) natural Peanut Butter

1 Whole Wheat Wrap

1 Banana

½ packet of Splenda

Method:

Add a bit of water to the protein powder in a bowl and stir until you get the same consistency as peanut butter

Add 1/2 packet of splenda and stir

Spread on whole wheat wrap

Cut up the banana and roll up inside the wrap

Macronutrients:

Protein: 32g

Carbs: 49g

Fats: 10g

Calories 435

Strawberry Fluff

Serves: 1

Preparation time: 5 minutes

Cooking time: None

Ingredients:

½ cup (125ml) or 1DL of Casein-Based Chocolate Protein Powder.

½ cup (125ml)or 1DL of Skimmed Milk.

About 300g of frozen Raspberries.

Method:

Put your protein powder in a bowl.

Pour your milk over the powder and mix it with a spoon

Put your berries in your microwave at low heating power for about five minutes. Be careful not to overdo it and unfreeze them completely because this may mess up your fluff.

When your berries are unfrozen put them in your bowl and mix everything again.

Take out your electronic mixer and mix for about 10 minutes.

The fluff is done when it has grown very big and fluffy.

Macronutrients:

Protein: 33g

Carbs: 30g

Fat: 6g

Calories: 306

Banana Flaxseed Muffins

Serves: 12

Preparation time: 10 minutes

Cooking time: 20 minutes

Ingredients:

½ cup (250ml Flax Seed

3 Bananas, mashed

¼ cup (63ml) Vegetable Oil

½ cup (125ml) Splenda

2 Egg Whites

1½ cups Vanilla Protein Powder

½ tsp (2,5ml) Baking Powder

½ tsp (2,5ml) Baking Soda

¼ cup (63ml) Whole Flax Seeds

Method:

Preheat oven to 350 F (180 C)

In a large mixing bowl, beat together bananas, oil, Splenda and egg whites.

Mix in the remaining ingredients, folding until smooth.

Lightly grease your muffin pan.

Spoon batter into prepared muffin pan.

Bake for 12-15 minutes or until a toothpick inserted into a muffin comes out clean.

Macronutrients (per serve):

Protein: 10g

Carbs: 10g

Fats: 3.5g

Calories: 105

Protein Pancakes/Strawberry Shortcake

Serves: 3

Preparation time: 10 minutes

Cooking time: 15 minutes

Ingredients:

2 scoops (60g) Strawberry Whey Protein Powder

¼ cup (63ml) Oats

¾ cup (190ml) Egg Whites

6oz (120g) fresh Strawberries

¼ cup (63ml) Mrs. Butterworth's SF Syrup

50g Reddi-Whip FF Whipped Cream

Method:

Blend the whites, whey, and oats in a blender and put in a cup.

Puree strawberries and syrup in blender, then put in a separate cup.

Heat a skillet to medium heat and coat with some non-stick spray.

Make the pancakes as you normally would. Pour over the strawberry puree and top with whipped cream.

Macronutrients (per serving):

Protein: 23g

Carbs: 17g

Fats: 1g

Calories: 170

Protein Lava Brownie

Serves: 1

Preparation time: 3 minutes

Cooking time: 1 minutes

Ingredients:

2 scoops (60g) Chocolate Protein Powder

2 Tbsp (60ml) Sugar Free Jello Pudding

2 Tbsp (60ml) Sugar Free Maple Syrup

1 Tbsp (15ml) extra Dark Cocoa

2 Egg Whites

2 packets of sweetener (splenda, stevia etc.)

Method:

Place all ingredients into mixing bowl.

Proceed to thoroughly stir, until a thick gooey consistency is achieved.

Microwave for 30 seconds.

Remove and stir.

Microwave for another 30 seconds.

Serve hot.

Macronutrients:

Protein: 60g

Carbs: 10g

Fats: 6g

Calories: 334

Protein Mousse Recipe

Serves: 6

Preparation time: 5 minutes

Cooking time: None

Ingredients:

1 Container (6 Ounces/170g) Plain Fat Free Greek Yogurt

½ Cup (125ml) Pure Pumpkin

½ Banana mashed

½ Tsp (2,5ml) Vanilla Extract

3 Tbsp (45ml) Powdered Peanut Butter

1½ Scoops (45g) Chocolate Protein Powder

2 Tbsp (30ml) Cocoa Powder

3 Packets Sweetener

Mini Graham Cracker Pie Crusts (Optional)

Method:

Combine all of your ingredients together into a bowl or food processor or mixing bowl

Pour your mix into a bowl or on top of your mini graham cracker pie crusts.

Macronutrients (per serve):

Protein: 11.5g

Carbs: 8.1g

Fat: 0.8g

Calories: 86.1

Protein Cookies and Cream Waffles

Serves: 1

Preparation time: 10 minutes

Cooking time: 10 minutes

Ingredients:

1 scoop (30g) Cellucor Cookies and Cream Whey

1 cup (250ml) Liquid Egg Whites

½ cup (125ml) Raw Oats

¼ Cup (63ml) Fiber One Cereal

1 tsp (5ml) Vanilla Extract

1 tsp (5ml) Ground Cinnamon

3 Tbsp (15ml) Unsweetened Baking Coco

Nonstick cooking spray

Method:

Start by heating up the waffle iron at a medium to high heat.

Grind the oats and fiber one cereal in a food processor, and set aside in a separate bowl.

Place the Liquid Egg Whites, and pour them in a blender and add in the fiber one and oat flour. Blend well,

Add the Cookies and Creme whey, baking coco, vanilla extract and blend well.

Spray the waffle iron with a nonstick spray and pour in batter. Sprinkle on the cinnamon (or mix in batter) and press down on the waffle iron. Flip every 2-3 minutes until cooked.

Suggested Toppings:

Peanut Butter

Fat Free Whipped Cream

SF Syrup

Macronutrients: (without toppings):

Protein: 52g

Carbs: 38g

Fat: 6g

Calories: 420

Gluten Free Protein Carrot Cake

Serves: 1

Preparation time: 10 minutes

Cooking time: 45 minutes

Ingredients:

½ cup (125ml) Vanilla Protein Powder

3 Tbsp (35ml) Coconut Flour

½ cup (125ml) gluten-free Oats

1½ cups (375ml) Almond Milk

2 small ripe Bananas, mashed

1 tsp (5ml) Baking Powder

1 (70g) Carrot, grated

1 (70g) Zucchini, grated

2 Tbsp (30ml) Walnuts

Method:

Preheat your oven to 350 F (180 C)

In a medium size mixing bowl combine the protein powder, coconut flour, oats, milk, baking powder, and bananas, and mix well.

With a spoon, mix in the grated carrots, zuchini, and walnuts.

Spray a medium sized bread tin with a nonstick spray and scoop the mixture into it.

Bake for 45 minutes, until cooked. Check by inserting a knife, the blade should be lean on withdrawal. Remove and cool completely before icing.

Mix 1 pack of Quark (250 grams) with 1/8 scoop (16g) of vanilla whey and 1 tsp (5ml) of freshly-shaven vanilla pods (optional).

Macronutrients:

Protein: 26g

Carbs: 22g

Fat: 6g

Calories: 246

Boston Cream Donut

Serves: 4

Preparation time: 15 minutes

Cooking time: 10 minutes

Ingredients:

1 medium Egg, separated

¼ cup (65ml) dry Quaker Old Fashioned Oats

2 large Egg Whites

1 tsp (5ml) Vanilla Extract

¾ tsp (3,5ml) Baking Powder

½ Tbsp (7,5ml) unsweetened Cocoa Powder

¼ tsp (1ml)) Xanthan Gum

1 Tbsp (15ml) Almond Meal Flour

¼ cup (63ml) Lowfat Cottage Cheese

2 tsp (10ml) Almond Milk - Unsweetened Original

½ scoop (20g) Vanilla Whey protein

3 packets Sugar in the Raw or Stevia in The Raw (Packet)

¾ tsp Butter extract

Method:

Preheat your oven to 350 F (180 C).

Grind the oats into a flour. Then add almond flour, vanilla whey protein, 3 egg whites, baking powder, vanilla extract, and 1 stevia packet.

Mix well Blend again.

Spray a donut pan with nonstick spray, and scoop batter into rings.

Bake for 10 minutes.

Topping

Cream, blend the lowfat cottage cheese, egg yolk, 1 stevia packet, 3/4 tsp butter extract, and xanthan gum.

Chocolate drizzle, mix the unsweetened cocoa powder, and unsweetened almond milk, and 1 stevia packet.

When the donuts are done, remove and top with the icing and chocolate.

Macronutrients (per serving):

Protein: 10g

Carbs: 7g

Fat: 3g

Calories: 94

Apple Pie Protein Donut

Serves: 5

Preparation time: 5 minutes

Cooking time: 5 minutes

Ingredients:

½ cup (125ml) dry Old Fashioned Oats

3 large Egg Whites

1ml Cinnamon

¼ tsp (2ml) Maple Extract

⅓ medium Apple, chopped

½ tsp (2ml) Baking Powder

4 tsp (20ml) Sugar Free Syrup

1 tsp (5ml) Vanilla Extract

¼ scoop (12g) Cellucor Cor-Performance Whey

1 packet Sugar in the Raw or Stevia in The Raw

Method:

Preheat your oven to 350 F (180 C).

Grind oats into a flour. Then add the whey protein, egg whites, baking powder, vanilla extract, maple extract, cinnamon, and 1 stevia packet. Blend again.

Add the chopped apple and swirl it into the batter.

Spray a donut pan with nonstick spray, and scoop batter into rings.

Bake10 minutes.

Topping:

3 Tbsp (45ml) sugar free syrup,

1 Tbsp (15ml) cinnamon swirl whey protein

Pinch of cinnamon (or vanilla)

Macronutrients (per serve):

Protein: 5g

Carbs: 9g

Fat: 1g

Calories: 55

Blueberry Protein Donuts

Serves: 4

Preparation time: 10 minutes

Cooking time: 10 minutes

Ingredients:

⅔ cup (165ml) dry Quaker Old Fashioned Oats

3 large Egg Whites

¼ tsp (1ml) Cinnamon

⅓ cup (85ml) Blueberries

½ tsp (2,5ml) Baking Powder

1 Tbsp (15ml) Bob's Red Mill Almond Meal Flour

½ tsp (2,5ml) Tone's Pure Almond Extract

½ tsp (2,5ml) McCormick Pure Vanilla Extract

½ scoop (20g) Dymatize Nutrition ISO 100 Hydrolyzed 100% Whey Protein Isolate

2 packets Sugar in the Raw or Stevia in The Raw

Method:

Preheat the oven to 350 F (180 C)

Grind the oats into a flour.

Add the rest of the ingredients except for the blueberries and blend again.

Swirl in the blueberries with a spoon.

Spray a donut pan with nonstick spray, and scoop batter into rings.

Bake for 10 minutes. take out and allow to cool.

Topping: (optional)

3 Tbsp (45ml) sugar free maple syrup, with

1 Tbsp (15ml)vanilla whey protein

Pinch of cinnamon

Macronutrients (per donut):

Protein: 7g

Carbs: 7g

Fat: 1.5g

Calories: 71

Chocolate Protein Donuts

Serves: multiple

Preparation time: 10 minutes

Cooking time: 15 minutes

Servings: 4

Ingredients:

1 tsp (5ml) Baking Powder

2 Tbsp (30 ml) Almond Meal Flour

⅓ cup (85ml)Almond Breeze Unsweetened Vanilla Milk

3 Tbsp (45ml) Smith Pure Pumpkin

½ scoop (15g) Pure Protein 100% Whey Protein - Frosty Chocolate

½ scoop (15g) Muscle Milk Light Vanilla Creme Protein Powder

4 Tbsp (60ml) Coconut Milk Yogurt - Vanilla

Method:

Preheat the oven to 350 F (180 C)

Batter:

Mix the almond meal, chocolate protein powder, unsweetened almond milk, chocolate extract, baking powder, and the pure pumpkin.

Spray a donut pan with nonstick spray, and scoop batter into rings.

Bake for 15 minutes. take out and allow to cool.

Frosting:

Mix the dairy free yogurt and vanilla protein powder. Pour over donuts once cooled. Top with chopped nuts or sprinkles.

Macronutrients (per serve):

Protein: 23g

Carbs: 26g

Fat: 13g

Calories: 294

Protein Packed Parfait

Serves: 1

Preparation time: 10 minutes

Cooking time: None

Ingredients:

1 scoop (30g) Gaspari ISO Fusion Protein Powder

1 Tbsp (15ml) Nescafe Instant Coffee

1 Tbsp (15ml) Cocoa powder

1 cup (250ml) Fage 0% Non-Fat Greek Yogurt

2 Tbsp (30ml) powdered Peanut Putter

⅓ cup (85ml) organic Granola

A few Fresh Blueberries

1 Tbsp (15ml) Dark Chocolate Chips

Method:

Place the granola into to a jar, glass, cup or bowl.

Add ⅓ cup (85ml) yogurt on top of the granola.

Mix ⅓ cup (85ml) yogurt with powdered peanut butter. Add to the jar.

Mix ⅓ cup (85ml) yogurt with protein powder, coffee, and cocoa powder. Add to the jar.

Top parfait with granola, chocolate chips, and blueberries.

Macronutrients:

Protein: 55 g

Carbs: 34 g

Fat: 9 g

Calories: 435

Coconut-Oat Bars

Serves: 2

Preparation time: 5 Minutes

Cooking time: None

Ingredients:

½ cup (125ml) Oats

½ cup (125ml) liquid Egg Whites

½ scoop (15g) Vanilla Protein

2 Tbsp (30ml) Reduced-Fat unsweetened Coconut Flakes

½ tsp (2.5ml) Coconut Extract

Cinnamon and Stevia to taste

Splash of unsweetened coconut milk

Method:

Preheat oven to 375 F (180 C)

Spray 8x8 pan with non-stick spray.

Blend all ingredients in a blender and pour into pan.

Bake for 15 minutes.

Cut into squares.

Macronutrients (per serve):

Protein: 22 g

Carbs: 21g

Fat: 3 g

Calories: 116

Cinnamon Scroll

Serves: Multiple

Preparation time: 5 Minutes

Cooking time: 15 Minutes

Ingredients:

Cake:

1/2 cup (125ml) liquid Egg Whites

1/2 cup (125ml) MyoFusion Cinnamon Roll Protein Powder

2 Tbsp (30ml) Oat Flour or instant Buckwheat

1 tsp (5ml) Baking Soda

1 Whole Egg

Frosting:

1/2 cup (125ml) Vanilla Whey

1/2 cup (125ml) Low Fat Greek yogurt

1 tsp (5ml) sugar-free maple syrup

Method:

Cake:

Preheat oven to 390 F (200 C)

Blend all ingredients for cake together.

Pour batter into a large brownie pan. Bake for 10-15 minutes.

When the cake is done, you'll notice it's pretty flat—kind of like a pancake—this is what we want. Allow to cool.

Frosting:

Combine all ingredients for frosting in a mixing bowl.

After cake is cooled, slice it into three or four strips and then coat each strip with frosting.

Sprinkle with cinnamon. Be sure to leave some frosting for topping.

Roll each cake strip to create the cinnamon roll.

Macronutrients:

Protein: 44g

Carbs: 11.4g

Fat: 4g

Calories: 290

Strawberry Cheesecake

Servings: 2

Preparation time: 15 Minutes

Cooking time: 45 Minutes

Ingredients:

Crust

¼ cup (62ml) Trader Joe's Just Almond Meal

¼ cup (62ml) shredded Dried Coconut (Shredded, Sweetened)

1 Tbsp (15ml) Coconut Oil

Filling

1 large Egg

1 large Egg White

1 Tbsp (15ml) Fresh Lemon Juice

1 cup (250 ml) 1% Lowfat Cottage Cheese, not packed

2 Tbsp (30ml) Cream Cheese (Fat Free)

1 scoop Body Fortress 100% Premium Vanilla Whey Protein

¾ cup (180ml) Liberte Greek Yogurt 0%

Topping

1 cup, (250ml) pureed Strawberries

2 Tbsp (30ml) Dried Chia Seeds

Method:

Preheat the oven to 190 C (375 F)

Crust:

Coat a pie dish with nonstick spray.

Mix almond meal, shredded coconut and coconut oil together in a mixing bowl.

Place in pie dish and press down to form crust.

Bake for 10 minutes at 190 C (375 F). Remove and let cool.

Filling:

Mix the egg, egg white, cottage cheese, Greek yogurt, fat free cream cheese, vanilla whey together in a mixing bowl, until smooth.

Add the fresh lemon juice and mix well.

Pour filling into the crust and even it out. Bake for 30-35 minutes at 190 C (375 F).

Take out and let cool.

Toppings:

Mix the strawberry puree and chia seeds together. Spread over the cheesecake.

Macronutrients (per serving):

Protein: 27g

Carbs: 40g

Fat: 10g

Calories: 365

Smoothies & Shakes

Chocolate Cookie Butter Mass Gain Smoothie

Meal Replacement Shake

Mass Gain Protein Shake (Without Protein Powder)

Iced Green Tea

Hard Gainer Shake

Breakfast Shake

Berry Blast Shake

Orange Creamsickle Protein Shake

Tuna Shake

Banana Bread Shake

Popeye Spinach Shake

Mocha Frappuccino

Pumpkin Protein Smoothie

Avocado Smoothie

Powder-less Protein Shake

Strawberry Cheesecake Protein Smoothie

Chocolate Cookie Butter Mass Gain Smoothie

Serves: 1

Preparation time: 5 Minutes

Cooking time: None

Ingredients:

2 scoops (60g) Chocolate Whey Powder

½ cup (125ml) Ice Water

¼ cup (62ml) Quick Oats

2 Tbsp (30ml) Cookie Butter

1/2 cup (125ml) frozen Greek Yogurt

Method:

Place all the ingredients in blender and blend to desired consistency. Consume immediately.

Macronutrients:

Protein: 52g

Carbs: 80g

Fat: 21g

Calories: 730

Meal Replacement Shake

Serves: 1

Preparation time: 5 Minutes

Cooking time: None

Ingredients:

1 cup (250ml) uncooked Oatmeal

2 scoops (60g)Vanilla protein

¼ tsp (2ml) Cinnamon

2 Tbsp (30ml) Sugar Free Maple Syrup

1 Tbsp (15ml) chopped Almonds

1½ cups (350ml) Water or Low Fat Milk

Method:

Place all the ingredients in blender and blend to desired consistency.
Consume immediately.

Macronutrients:

Protein: 68g

Carbs: 33g

Fat: 7g

Calories: 469

Mass Gain Protein Shake (Without Protein Powder)

Serves: 1

Preparation time: 5 Minutes

Cooking time: None

Ingredients:

4 Ice cubes

1 cup (250ml) Water

½ Egg Whites, Liquid

1 Banana, sliced

1 Tbsp (15ml) Peanut Butter

1 tub (130g) Nestlé Greek Yogurt

Method:

Place all the ingredients in blender and blend to desired consistency. Consume immediately.

Macronutrients:

Protein: 25g

Carbs: 55g

Fat: 12g

Calories: 428

Iced Green Tea

Serves: Multiple

Preparation time: 15 Minutes

Chilling time: 3 Hours

Ingredients:

4 cups (1ℓ) Water

2 Green Tea bags

Juice from 1 Lemon

2 Tbsp (30ml) of Honey (optional)

Sprig of Mint

Ice cubes

Method:

Bring the four cups of water to a boil, then pour into a pitcher with the tea bags.

Add the lemon juice, mint leaves, and honey into the tea, and let it steep for 10 minutes.

Remove the teabags and chill.

Add ice cubes and serve cold.

Macronutrients:

Protein: 1g

Carbs: 1g

Fat: 0g

Calories: 8

Hard Gainer Shake

Serves: 2

Preparation time: 10 Minutes

Cooking time: 2 Minutes

Ingredients:

1 cup (250ml) Peanut Butter

½ cup (125ml) Nutella

½ cup (125ml) Oats

2 cups (500ml) 2% Low Fat Milk

1 Banana, sliced

1 tsp (5ml) Cinnamon

Method:

Mix the oats, cinnamon and 1 cup of milk in a microwave proof bowl, and cook for 1minute on high. Remove, stir and cook for another minute.

Scoop the cooked oatmeal mixture into a blender, and blend until smooth.

Add the peanut butter, Nutella, banana and remaining cup of milk, and blend until smooth.

Consume immediately.

Macronutrients (per serve):

Protein: 47g

Carbs: 117g

Fat: 94g

Calories: 1502

Breakfast Shake

Serves: 1

Preparation time: 5 Minutes

Cooking time: None

Ingredients:

2 scoops (60g) Vanilla or Chocolate Protein Powder

1 Banana sliced

¼ cup (62ml) frozen Blueberries

¼ cup (62ml) frozen Black Cherries

¼ cup (62ml) shredded Coconut

⅓ tsp (2ml) Lemon Juice

Method:

Place all the ingredients in blender and blend to desired consistency. Consume immediately.

Macronutrients:

Protein: 65g

Carbs: 30g

Fat: 7g

Calories: 445

Berry Blast Shake

Serves: 2

Preparation time: 5 Minutes

Cooking time: None

Ingredients:

5 Ice cubes

1 cup (250ml) Blueberries

¼ cup (62ml) chopped Cashews

¼ cup (62ml) sliced Almonds

½ cup (125ml) Full-Fat Cottage Cheese

4 scoops (120g) of Vanilla Protein Powder

2 cups (500ml) Milk

¼ tsp (1ml) ground Cinnamon

1 Banana, sliced

1 Tbsp (5ml) Peanut Butter

Method:

Place all the ingredients in blender and blend to desired consistency. Consume immediately.

Macronutrients (per serve):

Protein: 73g

Carbs: 29g

Fat: 18g

Calories: 570

Orange Creamsickle Protein Shake

Serves: 1

Preparation time: 5 Minutes

Cooking time: None

Ingredients:

1 cup (250ml) Ice

1 cup (250ml) Orange Juice

1 scoop (30g) Vanilla Whey

1 tsp (5ml) Vanilla Extract

2 Tbsp (30ml) Non Fat Plain Greek Yogurt

Method:

Place all the ingredients in blender and blend to desired consistency. Consume immediately.

Macronutrients:

Protein: 33g

Carbs: 25g

Fat: 3g

Calories: 259

Tuna Shake

Serves: 1

Preparation time: 5 Minutes

Cooking time: None

Ingredients:

2 6oz cans (340g) Tuna, drained

2 cups (500ml) Water

4 Large Ice cubes

Method:

Place all the ingredients in blender and blend to desired consistency. Consume immediately.

Macronutrients:

Protein: 80g

Carbs: 4g

Fat: 0g

Calories: 336

Banana Bread Shake

Serves: 1

Preparation time: 5 Minutes

Cooking time: None

Ingredients:

2 scoops (60g) Vanilla Whey Protein

1 Banana, peeled and sliced

½ cup (125ml) Quaker Oatmeal (cooked in water)

½ cup (125ml) Bran Flakes

1½ cup (350ml) Water

30g of Dextrose (Only if consumed post-workout)

Method:

Place all the ingredients in blender and blend to desired consistency. Consume immediately.

Macronutrients:

Protein: 56g

Carbs: 64g (34 without Dextrose)

Fat: 2g

Calories: 498

Popeye Spinach Shake

Serves: 1

Preparation time: 5 Minutes

Cooking time: None

Ingredients:

1½ cups (375ml) Water

1 - 1½ cups (375ml) leafy Spinach

2 Tbsp (30ml) Almond Butter

2 scoops (30g) Whey Protein

4 cubes Ice

Method:

Place all the ingredients in blender and blend to desired consistency. Consume immediately.

Macronutrients:

Protein: 56g

Carbs: 10g

Fat: 19g

Calories: 424

Mocha Frappuccino

Serves: 1

Preparation time: 5 Minutes

Cooking time: None

Ingredients:

1 tsp (5ml) instant coffee granules of your choice

1 scoop (30g) Chocolate Whey Protein

1½ cup (375 ml) Crushed Ice = 10-15 ice cubes

1 cup (250ml)Skimmed Milk

2-3 packs Splenda

Method:

Place all the ingredients in blender and blend to desired consistency. Consume immediately.

Macronutrients:

Protein: 43g

Carbs: 8g

Fat: 2g

Calories: 222

Pumpkin Protein Smoothie

Serves: 1

Preparation time: 5 Minutes

Cooking time: None

Ingredients:

1½ scoops (45g) Double Chocolate Whey

½ Can Libby's Canned Pumpkin Puree

1 Packet Splenda or Honey

½ cup (125ml) Water

6 Ice cubes

Method:

Place all the ingredients in blender and blend to desired consistency.
Consume immediately.

Macronutrients:

Protein: 40g

Carbs: 22.5g

Fat: 1.5g

Calories: 260

Avocado Smoothie

Serves: 2

Preparation time: 5 Minutes

Cooking time: None

Ingredients:

1 Medium Avocado, peeled and diced

1 cup (250ml) Almond Milk

1 tsp (5ml) Honey

¼ - ½ tsp (2-2,5ml) Vanilla Extract

Method:

Place all the ingredients in blender and blend to desired consistency. Consume immediately.

Macronutrients:

Protein: 3g

Carbs: 17g

Fat: 13g

Calories: 180

Powder-less Protein Shake

Serves: 1

Preparation time: 10 Minutes

Cooking time: None

Ingredients:

¾ Cup (190ml) Sugar Free Vanilla Coconut Milk (or Milk Substitute)

½ tsp (2,5ml)Vanilla Extract

½ tsp (2,5ml) Ground Cinnamon

1 Tub (5.3 Ounces/150g) Vanilla Fat Free Greek Yogurt

¼ cup (62ml) Fat Free Cottage Cheese

1 Tbsp (15ml) Peanut Butter

9 Tbsp (135ml) Liquid Egg Whites

1 Tbsp (15ml) Instant Sugar Free Fat Free Vanilla Pudding

Ice (Optional)

Method:

Place all the ingredients in blender and blend to desired consistency.
Consume immediately.

Macronutrients:

Protein: 31g

Carbs: 27g

Fat: 7g

Calories: 295

Strawberry Cheesecake Protein Smoothie

Serves: 1

Preparation time: 10 Minutes

Cooking time: None

Ingredients:

1 cup (250ml) Sugar Free Vanilla Coconut Milk (or milk substitute)

3 Tbsp (45ml) Liquid Egg Whites

1 Tbsp (15ml) Instant Sugar Free Fat Free Cheesecake Jello

1 cup (250ml) Halved Strawberries

1/2 cup (125ml) Fat Free Cottage Cheese

1½ scoops (45g) Strawberry or Vanilla Protein Powder

1/2 tsp (5ml)Vanilla Extract

1 cup (250ml) Ice

Method:

Place all the ingredients in blender and blend to desired consistency. Consume immediately.

Macronutrients:

Protein: 59g

Carbs: 30g

Fat: 6g

Calories: 410

Sides

Low Calorie Chocolate Sauce

Athlete Trail Mix

High Protein Ranch Sauce

Tuna Dip

Shrimp Ceviche

Shrimp Sliders

Turkey-Wrapped Asparagus

Cupcake Frosting

Scallop Cerviche

Cinnamon Sweet Potato Fries

Clean Protein Nutella Spread

Low Calorie Chocolate Sauce

Serves: multiple

Preparation time: 5 Minutes

Cooking time: None

Ingredients:

5g Cocoa or powdered Hot Chocolate of your choice

2 tsp (10ml) Canderel/Splenda/Sweetener of choice

½ tsp (2,5ml)Vanilla Extract.

½ Tsp (2,5ml) Xanthan Gum.

Small amount of boiling Water

Method:

Combine the cocoa, sweetner and Xanthan gum in a cup.

Add the vanilla extract and smix well.

Add increments of boiling water to the mixture, until the desired consistency is obtained – should you add too much water, add a small amount of Xanthan gum.

Leave to cool/set, or use immediately.

Macronutrients:

Protein: 1g

Carbs: 0g

Fat: 4g

Calories: 28

Athlete Trail Mix

Serves: multiple

Preparation time: 5 Minutes

Cooking time: None

Ingredients:

½ cup (125ml) Dairy free, gluten free chocolate chips

½ cup (125ml) Pumpkin seeds

½ cup (125ml) Sunflower seeds

½ cup (125ml) Banana Chips

½ cup (125ml) Dried Cranberries

½ cup (125ml) Shredded Coconut

(Or whichever dried fruits/nuts you prefer!)

Method:

Place all ingredients in a mixing bowl and mix well.

Seal in an airtight container, or pack into small snack-sized ziplock bags.

Snack on as desired.

Macronutrients:

Macronutrient breakdown and total number of calories is hard to determine with trail mix, however I recommend experimenting with your favourite seeds and nuts, and obtaining a baseline from these calories.

High Protein Ranch Sauce

Servings: Multiple

Preparation time: 10 Minutes

Cooking time: None

Ingredients:

6oz (170g) Fat Free Plain Greek Yogurt

9 Tbsp (135ml) Fat Free Sour Cream

¼ tsp (2ml) Dill, chopped

1 tsp (5ml) Parsley, chopped

3/4 tsp (3ml) Salt

½ tsp (2,5ml) Onion Powder

¼ tsp (2ml) Garlic Powder

¼ tsp(2ml) Black Pepper

Water (until desired consistency)

1/2 Scoop (15g) Natural Flavored Protein Powder (optional)

Method:

Place all of the ingredients in a mixing bowl and mix well.

Add in water until the sauce has obtained your desired consistency (the less water you use the creamier it'll be).

Add a natural flavored protein powder if you want more protein.

Macronutrients:

Protein: 34g

Carbs: 23g

Fat: 0g

Calories: 228

Tuna Dip

Servings: Multiple

Preparation time: 5 Minutes

Cooking time: None

Ingredients:

1 Can (5 Ounces/142g) Tuna

⅓ Packet Ranch Dip

2 Tbsp (30ml) Flax Seed

1 Container (6 Ounces/170g) Plain Fat Free Greek Yogurt

Method:

Drain your can of Tuna.

Place in a mixing bowl, add the ranch dip, flax seed and yogurt and mix well.

Serve immediately with snacks.

Macronutrients:

Protein: 47g

Carbs:16g

Fat: 5g

Calories: 297

Shrimp Ceviche

Servings: 4

Preparation time: 5 Minutes

Cooking time: None

Ingredients:

½ lb (225g) Large shrimp, cooked, peeled and chopped

½ cup (125ml) Cherry Tomatoes, sliced

¼ Red Onion, sliced

¼ cup (62ml) Cilantro, chopped

½ Avocado, chopped

Juice of 1 Lime

Salt and Pepper, to taste

Method:

Add ingredients to a medium bowl.

Toss and refrigerate before serving.

Macronutrients (per serving):

Protein: 12.5g

Carbs: 5.5g

Fat: 4.4g

Calories: 111

Shrimp Sliders

Servings: 3

Preparation time: 5 Minutes

Cooking time: None

Ingredients:

6 oz (170g) raw Shrimp, de-veined and peeled

3 Ozery Bakery multigrain slider buns

½ cup (125ml) Bell Pepper, diced

1 Roma Tomato, sliced

Lettuce leaves

½ Tbsp (7,5ml) Kelapo Coconut oil or use the spray

Seasonings:

Onion powder,

Garlic powder,

Pepper,

Cumin

Method:

Wash and remove all tails and peel the raw shrimp and Dry the shrimp with a paper towel.

Add the shrimp to a blender and pulse blend until a chunky, thick sticky paste is achieved.

Remove the shrimp from the food processor and season with your choice of seasonings.

Mix using your hands, and form three equal sized patties.

Heat a skillet on medium heat and add the Kelapo coconut oil. (If you are placing the shrimp on the grill, be sure to grease the rack.)

Place the shrimp sliders on the skillet and cook until the shrimp patties turn pink.

Assemble the sliders using a small leaf of lettuce and a slice of Roma tomato.

Serve immediately.

Macronutrients (per serving):

Serving size 1 slider

Protein: 14g

Carbs:13g

Fat: 2g

Calories: 135

Turkey-Wrapped Asparagus

Servings: 12

Preparation time: 10 Minutes

Cooking time: 10 Minutes

Ingredients:

A bundle of thick spears of Asparagus (roughly 12)

24oz (600g) Turkey Lunchmeat, sliced thinly

Kelapo Coconut Oil

Seasonings (optional):

Bragg's Liquid Aminos,

Garlic powder,

Onion powder

Instructions:

Preheat oven to 450 F (220 C)

Spray a baking sheet with a nonstick spray

Chop bottom stems off asparagus.

Wrap each asparagus with 2 oz of sliced turkey lunch meat.

Heat a skillet over a medium-high flame and spray with Kelapo coconut oil.

Place the wrapped asparagus in the skillet with the turkey flap end down.

Sear the wrapped asparagus.

While cooking, add seasoning.

Once all sides of the turkey are seared, remove from the skillet.

Place the wrapped asparagus in the oven on a baking sheet and bake in the oven for 4-5 minutes.

Serve warm.

Macronutrients (per serving):

Serving size: One asparagus wrap

Protein:12g

Carbs: 2g

Fat: 1g

Calories: 66

Cupcake Frosting

Servings: Multiple

Preparation time: 5 Minutes

Cooking time: None

Ingredients:

2 scoops casein protein powder (½ - ¾ cup, depending on desired thickness)

1 cup (250ml) Greek yogurt

5 Tbsp (75ml) Milk

Method:

Place the protein powder and yogurt together in a bowl, and mix.

Stir in one tablespoon of milk at a time, until the mixture acquires a frosting like texture. It should be creamy and not overly runny. Feel free to add more casein if you want thicker frosting, or more yogurt if you want it creamier.

When casein mixture is ready, use it to frost your cooled muffins. You can either use a knife to spread it, or put the frosting in a Ziploc bag, cut off a corner, and use it as a frosting bag.

Macronutrients:

Protein: 75g

Carbs: 5g

Fat: 5g

Calories:

Scallop Cerviche

Serves: 3

Preparation time: Overnight

Cooking time: None

Ingredients:

1 lb (450g) Bay Scallops (these are small scallops, roughly the size of a marble)

Juice of 6 Limes (enough to cover the scallops – you can use lemons if you prefer)

½ large Red Onion chopped

1 medium sized Tomato

1 stalk of Celery

2 Tbsp (30ml) of Capers

2 Tbsp (30ml) Olive Oil

Pinch of Sea Salt

1 tsp (5ml) ground Black Pepper (or to taste)

Method:

Place the scallops into a shallow bowl and squeeze the juice from the limes over the scallops.

Cover and refrigerate for 4-8 hours (overnight).

Remove from the refrigerator, and drain off most of the limejuice.

Dice the onion, tomato, and celery, and add it to the scallops along with the capers, salt, olive oil and pepper.

Refrigerate for another hour and serve cold.

Macronutrients (per serving):

Protein: 26g

Carbs: 7g

Fat: 10g

Calories: 241

Cinnamon Sweet Potato Fries

Serves: 1

Preparation time: 10 Minutes

Cooking time: 20 Minutes

Ingredients:

½ tbsp (7.5ml) Cinnamon

250 g Sweet Potato

¼ cup (62ml) Extra Virgin Olive Oil

½ scoop (15g) Cellucor Cor-Performance Whey

Method:

Preheat your oven to 425 F (200 C)

Wash and dry your sweet potato, peel if preferred.

Coat a baking tray with nonstick cooking spray.

Slice into fries – ensure that they are all about the same width.

Place the olive oil and Cinnamon Swirl protein in a mixing bowl, and mix well.

Coat all your fries and place on a baking sheet, ensure that the fries are evenly spaced.

Sprinkle with cinnamon.

Bake for 15-20 minutes at depending on how thick your fries are.

Check every 5 minutes or so. You may want to flip them ½ or ¾ the way through.

Serve hot

Macronutrients (per serving):

Protein: 8g

Carbs: 27g

Fat: 27g

Calories: 383

Clean Protein Nutella Spread

Serves: Multiple

Preparation time: 10 Minutes

Cooking time: 10 Minutes

Ingredients:

2 cups (500ml) Raw Hazelnuts

1½ tbsp (22.5ml) pure Vanilla Extract

¼ cup (63ml) Cacao Powder

¼ cup (63ml) Rice Malt Syrup (or other sweetener)

½ cup (125ml) of unsweetened Almond Milk

Method:

Preheat your oven to Preheat oven to 200 F (1200 C)

Place the hazelnuts on a baking sheet and roast for 10 minutes.

Remove from the oven and allow to cool.

Using a paper towel, rub the hazelnuts together to remove their darkened skin.

Blend the nuts in a food processor until smooth and buttery.

Add the Cacao powder, sweetener, vanilla extract and almond milk,

Blend well until smooth.

Store in an airtight jar or container in a cool place until ready to use.

Macronutrients:

Protein: 38g

Carbs: 50g

Fat: 90g

Calories: 1162

Conclusion

I hope these recipes will serve you well on the way to achieving your health and fitness goals. Once you've got these recipes mastered don't be shy to add extra ingredients and flavours, as well as alter the amount of protein/carbohydrates based ingredients in each dish to better suit your calorie and macronutrient goals.

I'd love to hear your success stories with these recipes, and your overall thoughts on the Flexible Dieting Cook Book – feel free to submit a review via Amazon.

Happy cooking!

Scott James

Also by Scott James

Flexible Dieting 101: Eat the Foods you Love and Achieve the Body of your Dreams!

Click here to view Flexible Dieting 101 on Amazon.com

The Bicep Workout Bible: Get Huge Arms, a Complete Guide to Building Shredded Bicep Muscles

Click here to view the Bicep Workout Bible on Amazon.com

Made in the USA
Middletown, DE
10 May 2018